CONSTRUCTION CONTRACTS DEMYSTIFIED

Guiding Young Entrepreneurs and Students
Through the Maze of Construction Contracts

MANISH MOHANDAS

STARDOM BOOKS

www.StardomBooks.com

STARDOM BOOKS
112 Bordeaux Ct.
Coppell, TX 75019, USA

FIRST EDITION MARCH 2024

STARDOM BOOKS, LLC.
112 Bordeaux Ct. Coppell, TX 75019, USA

www.stardombooks.com

Stardom Books, United States
Stardom Alliance, India

CONSTRUCTION CONTRACTS DEMYSTIFIED
Guiding Young Entrepreneurs and Students Through the Maze of Construction Contracts

Manish Mohandas

p. 261
cm. 13.5 X 21.5

Category:
LAW021000 Law : Contracts
BUS010000 Business & Economics : Business Law
BUS070160 Business & Economics :
Industries - Construction

ISBN: 978-1-957456-43-0

DEDICATION

This book is dedicated to my family who has inspired me to embark on this journey. Apart from my family, I wish to dedicate this book to all students and young entrepreneurs who wish to have a basic understanding of Contracts.

CONTENTS

Acknowledgments   i

Introduction   1

1   Overall Contract Process   7

2   Major Terms of Any Agreement   39

3   Standard Forms of Contracts   77

4   FIDIC Red Book 1999 - A Closer Look   115

5   Know Your Client or Vendor   177

7   Conclusion   245

8   References   247

9   About the Author   249

ACKNOWLEDGMENTS

This book is dedicated to my family who has inspired me to embark on this journey. Apart from my family, I also wish to thank all my peers, colleagues, contractors, consultants, suppliers and other such vendors from India, United Arab Emirates (UAE), Sri Lanka and Maldives who have inspired me in multiple ways during my professional interactions with them in these countries.

Further, I wish to thank the Directors and Senior Management of VMS Consultants, Mumbai, India; Hindustan Construction Company Ltd, Mumbai, India, ETA ASCON, Dubai, UAE; Aldar Laing O'Rourke, Abu Dhabi, UAE; Rustomjee, Mumbai, India; Tata Housing, Mumbai, India and more recently the Karle Group, Bengaluru, India for having provided me with the opportunity to work on multiple interesting and challenging assignments which has motivated me to write down my thoughts on the subject of Contract management.

I have also been inspired and motivated by over 300 plus feedback and suggestions received from across the world from members of the Project Management Institute (PMI), USA who have reviewed two of my publications on PMI on the subject.

I also acknowledge the contributions of various experts on the subject of contracts whose publications have inspired me. A full list of all references which have been referred in the preparation of this book is enclosed in the reference section of this book.

INTRODUCTION

A building, no matter how it looks, is the result of somebody's dream. A mall or a shopping center is the result of an entrepreneur's dream; likewise, a house is a result of a person's hard work and patience. Everybody knows for a fact that a building is made up of cement and stones. However, do you know that there are several other steps in the process?

In the construction of modern urban landscapes, there exists an intricate dance between the visionary buyer and the industrious seller, a collection of blueprints and bulldozers, of dreams and dedication. In this book we embark on a journey through the labyrinthine world of construction tendering, meticulous documents, strategic negotiations, and seemingly innocuous clauses that possess the latent power to shape the destiny of projects.

It all starts with a special document called the tender document. This document holds the dreams and hopes of the project. It's like a loud call to the people who build things, asking them to help make big buildings. Making this document is not a rushed job. It's done very carefully. The person who wants the building (the buyer) writes down exactly what they want. They say how big it should be, what it should be made of, and when it should be finished. They have to be

1

very clear, so there's no confusion. It's like painting a picture, and every detail has to be just right.

The person who will build the project (we call them the seller or the Contractor) takes a very close look at the tender document. They read every word and measure everything carefully. This is the very first important step, because in construction (like any other industry), being exact is super important. It's like when a skilled artist looks at a canvas to see if it's good enough. The seller checks the tender document to see if they can do the job well. They ask themselves: Can they do what the buyer wants? Can they finish it on time without making any sacrifices in quality? These are some of the most important questions for the seller. It's like a test to see if they're really up for the job. This book will help you find answers to these questions. You will also get to know about the questions which you have to ask as well.

Once the tender document is given to possible builders, a lot of offers and ideas come pouring in. In this situation, the person who wants the building (we call them the buyer) becomes like an expert judge. They carefully look at each offer, just like someone who knows a lot about something valuable. They don't just think about money. They also think about whether the builder has done good work before and if they have experience in building things. In this dance of doing business and making things, trust is even more important than money. It's like a kind of priceless treasure.

Once the right builders are chosen, it's time for them and the person who wants the building (buyer) to have a talk about the technical and money parts. This is like the second important part of the whole process. It's a bit like an act where they share their thoughts and what matters most to them. The builder, who knows a lot about materials and workers, explains how they see the project working. They talk about all the small details that need to be done to make it successful. At the same time, the buyer, who has their own ideas and budget limits, tries to find a way to make everyone's wishes come true while also being realistic. It's like finding a way to make a dream come true within the limits of what's possible.

In the middle of these talks, boilerplate clauses become the unsung heroes. They act like a safety net, supporting the whole project quietly in the background. Even though they might seem like regular rules hidden in the small print, they actually have the power to change how things go in the construction project. Clauses about responsibility for accidents, dealing with big unexpected events, and settling disagreements or disputes are all part of these special rules. Right now, they might not seem important, but if something unexpected happens, they step in to help the stakeholders who are associated with the building project. They're like a safety net for the whole project, ready to provide protection and a way to solve problems for both sides.

However, it's the little, seemingly unimportant details that can make a big difference. For example, a rule about bad weather delays might seem small, but when a big storm hits, it can seriously affect the project's schedule. Similarly, forgetting to define changes in the plan might not seem like a big deal, until things start to change, causing a bunch of problems. These quiet rules, hidden in the Contract documents, show how careful planning in contracts is really important.

In this book, we'll take a closer look at every step in this complicated process. From creating the tender document to finishing the construction, each step is very important and can lead to success. This book is a special contribution to the world of construction and procurement.

These are the people who create the important documents and have the important talks, bringing buildings to life. It's a guide for anyone interested, whether you're just starting out or have been doing this for a while.

INTRODUCTION

It invites everyone to be a part of the amazing process of making modern marvels happen. Brace yourself up as we delve into the innermost layers of this wonderful journey of crafting skyscrapers.

Please keep in mind that:

1. This book is not a substitute for expert legal opinions.

2. This book is a compilation of various aspects of construction contracts some of which are directly contributed by the author and some are compiled from the rich and diverse materials which have been published earlier by individuals who are passionate about the subject.

3. It aims at providing the reader with enough information to help in contract discussions and negotiations, and to arrive at watertight contract agreements for their respective businesses.

Given below are a few pain points that could be experienced by the reader:

a) Strains in relationships with clients and vendors due to poor understanding of contracts and agreements

b) Losses being incurred due to incorrect pricing in contracts, extended period of contracts etc

c) Not clearly understanding the Contracts or agreements

d) Perhaps also not exactly knowing who is their Client or vendor (legal position)

This book should help the readers focus on other aspects of their business or profession by providing them an understanding of contracts to the extent that they need to be aware of.

Lastly, it is also an attempt to improve the ease of doing business between companies or individuals in line with the Indian governments initiative to improve India's global position on the ease of doing business ranking.

It is also an attempt to bring about a better understanding of contracts to help reduce disputes and thereby maintain healthy business relationships.

CHAPTER 1:

OVERALL CONTRACT PROCESS

Bob[1] wants to build his dream house and is seeking an individual or organization to design and construct it. After receiving recommendations from friends and relatives, Bob decides to hire Carl Constructions LLP for the project.

However, before entering into an agreement, there are several important considerations to address.

Can Bob directly enter into an agreement with Carl Constructions LLP, or are there specific steps he needs to take? Is Carl Constructions LLP genuinely interested in building Bob's dream house? How well does Bob know the company, and has he effectively communicated his requirements?

This chapter explores the necessary measures Bob should take to clearly communicate his needs and ensure that Carl Constructions LLP can complete the project within the desired timeframe and budget.

---

[1] Bob and Carl Constructions LLP are only fictitious names and do not resemble any person

Additionally, it addresses potential scenarios such as project delays, construction defects, and other risks.

On the other hand, it's crucial to consider Carl Constructions LLP's understanding of Bob as a client. Have they comprehended Bob's requirements sufficiently? If Carl Constructions LLP does not win the project bid, will Bob reimburse the costs incurred during the bidding.

process? Will Bob pay them promptly as a client, and does he have the necessary funds to finance the construction? What if Bob decides to halt construction midway or change his requirements during the project? Who bears the risk of material price escalations? Furthermore, it's essential to ensure that Bob has obtained all the necessary statutory clearances for his proposed construction site. Lastly, what happens if Bob goes bankrupt during the construction process?

In this chapter, we will examine the steps that both the Buyer (Bob) and the Seller (Carl Constructions LLP) need to take. Although we will refer to Bob as the Buyer and Carl Constructions LLP as the Seller or Contractor, the principles discussed apply to any complex project in any industry.

Transition to Tender Document Preparation:

Once Bob has finalized his decision to construct his dream house, the next step is to consolidate all his thoughts and requirements into a formal document called the Tender Document. The Tender Document typically includes various sections, as shown in Table 1:

Section 1 - Conditions of contract	Section 2 - Technical Section	Section 3 - Other documents
Expression of Interest (EOI)	Technical specifications	Logistics Plan
Notice Inviting Tenders	Bill of quantities	Environment, Health and Safety requirements
Instructions to Bidders (ITB)	Drawings	Any other special requirements of the Buyer
General Conditions of Contract (GCC)	Program expectations	
Particular Conditions of Contract (PCC)	Quality expectations	

(Table- 1)

Each section plays a crucial role, and their importance will be discussed in subsequent chapters.

Now, Bob has the option to either create the tender document himself or seek the services of a professional. For smaller projects, Bob can prepare the document independently by himself. However, for larger and more complex projects, it is recommended to avail the assistance of a professional. This leads us to two important steps:

Step 1 – Appoint a professional for preparing the tender document.

Step 2 – Prepare the tender document.

Next, Bob has received recommendations for potential contractors from his friends and relatives. However, he is uncertain about their capabilities. How can Bob ensure that he selects the right contractor? Are there other contractors available in the market beyond the recommendations he received? This brings us to the next set of steps: Bidder Identification, Bidder Rating, and Bidder Shortlisting. These steps help Bob identify the most suitable contractor for his project.

Step 3 - Bidder identification involves the process of identifying potential Sellers (Contractors) who may be interested in providing services to the Buyer (in this case, construction of the dream house). There are various methods for bidder identification, including utilizing existing databases, newspaper advertisements, websites, social media, referrals, and company websites, among other sources.

Step 4 - Bidder rating is the process of assigning a rating to the identified bidders based on a set of parameters and their respective weightages, which the Buyer can determine. A sample rating table is provided in Table 2:

Sr no	Criteria	Weightage	Bidder 1		Bidder 2		Bidder 3	
			Rating	Score	Rating	Score	Rating	Score
1	Technical	10%						
2	Financial	20%						
3	Resources	10%						
4	Quality	20%						
5	EHS**	20%						
6	Statutory Compliances	10%						
7	Litigation History	10%						
	Total	100%						

**EHS – Environment, Health and Safety
Above percentages are indicative and need to be adjusted based on specific organizational needs

(Table-2)

10

The Buyer can establish qualifying criteria for the rating. For instance, the Buyer may decide not to proceed further with any bidder whose weighted average score is below 50%.

Step 5 - Bidder shortlisting involves selecting bidders who meet the qualifying criteria and considering bid capacity evaluation for the specific project. A sample bid capacity calculation is provided as follows:

Bid Capacity:

Bid capacity is a calculation which indicates if the Bidder is capable of executing the Client's works in the specified time considering the Bidder's other commitments during the same period during which the Client's works have to be executed. The bidder who meets the minimum qualifying criteria will be eligible for further consideration of bids only if their available bid capacity exceeds the estimated value of the project stated in the Notice Inviting Tender. The available bid capacity can be calculated as follows:

Assessed available bid capacity $= A \times N \times 2 - B$

Where:

N = number of years prescribed for project/contract completion

A = maximum value of works executed by the bidder in one year during the last five years

B = value of bidder's existing commitments and ongoing works to be completed during the proposed project completion period

Please refer to Table 3 for a sample format to collect data for bid capacity calculation.

OVERALL CONTRACT PROCESS

PROFORMA-VI

DETAILS OF ON-GOING/EXISTING WORKS

Sl. No.	Description of the Work with Contract No.	Name and address of the Employer With Contact No.	Date of award	Stipulated date of completion	Value of work as per order (Rs. in lacs)	Value of work completed so far (Rs. in lacs)	Anticipated date of Completion of work	Any other relevant information

Note: The copies of certificates of ongoing-awarded works issued by the owner shall be attached.

(Table-3)

The Buyer has now documented their requirements and identified potential sellers. However, the Buyer still needs to ascertain if the bidders are genuinely interested in providing the services within the specified timelines and other relevant factors. To determine this, it is recommended to use an Expression of Interest (EOI), which brings us to Step 6.

Expression of Interest (EOI):

Step 6 - An expression of interest is a communication made by a bidder (potential seller) in response to a notification, advertisement, or any other form of communication by the Buyer regarding the supply of goods or services. Requesting expressions of interest allows the Buyer to compile a list of potential suppliers that may be invited to tender. The methods for requesting expressions of interest can vary, such as online platforms or printed publications like newspapers.

12

A communication requesting expressions of interest typically includes:

a) A brief introduction of the Buyer
b) Description of the contract, including volume and size
c) Contract type and conditions
d) Program of works with specific milestones
e) Bid submission address and deadlines
f) Details of the information required in the expression of interest
g) Buyer's contact details
h) Bidder description, including financial information
i) Relevant bidder experience and technical capacity
j) Bidder staff experience and availability
k) Bidder's previous client references

Using a predefined template for bidders to submit their responses ensures consistency and facilitates easy comparison. The information submitted in an expression of interest helps the Buyer narrow down the number of bidders to be invited for tender submissions. On larger projects, there may be additional pre-qualification processes following the submission of expressions of interest, which could involve site visits, financial assessments, assessments of litigation history, and other criteria. It is advisable to seek expressions of interest as early as possible, particularly to avoid potential delays in the tender process. In agile procurement methods, these timelines may vary.

An Expression of Interest (EOI) is a valuable tool used by the Buyer to initiate a project and evaluate a Bidder's interest, while also obtaining useful information from interested Bidders. It serves multiple purposes, some of which are described below:

1. Project Vision:

During the pre-project development stage, it is important to establish a clear vision for the project that addresses a specific need or demand. An EOI not only assesses the availability of suitable Bidders for the project but also serves as a means to gather feedback and refine the

Buyer's vision to meet the needs of the target end user.

2. Interest generation and market research:

In many cases, an EOI acts as a market research tool. By assessing the project's ability to attract interested parties, the EOI stimulates interest and helps identify qualified organizations and individuals who may respond to the opportunity in later stages of the procurement process.

3. Aligning Project Requirements and Bidder Capacity:

The EOI process minimizes gaps by aligning project requirements with the capacity of the Bidders. On one hand, it simplifies the identification of eligible Bidders for the competitive selection process, confirming if they meet the eligibility requirements and possess the financial capacity to participate. On the other hand, the EOI provides an opportunity to gauge Bidder interests and adjust the project requirements accordingly for the subsequent phases of the procurement process.

4. Procurement Type:

In certain projects, it may not be suitable to procure organizations or individuals through the standard process of inviting proposals from a predetermined list. In such cases, an EOI can be used as a filter to manage potential Bidders who exceed the optimal number for a selected list of proposals or tenders. It ensures that interested parties meet the minimum pre-qualification criteria for the required services and also provides an opportunity for interested Bidders to form strategic alliances, where applicable.

5. When to Use an Expression of Interest:

An EOI is most commonly used during the initial stages of a project to assess interest, facilitate potential alliances, or refine the project's vision based on feedback from information sessions and written EOIs.

It can serve as a precursor to a feasibility study or be used within a feasibility study to carry out market research and contribute to project appraisal.

The Step-by-Step Expression of Interest Process:

1. Review Project Context:

To make the EOI process effective and user-friendly, it is crucial to thoroughly review the project's background research. Ensure the EOI document provides a clear and accurate description of the project vision, along with practical information that attracts responses from target Bidders. Proposed project timelines should be achievable, as a Bidder's response may be based on these timelines.

2. Draft the Expression of Interest:

A well-prepared EOI document minimizes the effort and documentation required of respondents, encouraging their participation. It is important to note that the EOI process is not a selection process but an opportunity for potential Bidders to contribute to project planning. The EOI should address the following aspects:

a) An overview of the opportunity and its intended audience.
b) The Project: Background, Vision, Timeline, Additional materials (e.g., floor plans, site plans, research documents).
c) Review Criteria: List and describe the criteria to be used by the Buyer's team to review responses. These are not selection criteria and may be optional.
d) Submission Requirements: Eligibility Requirements, Information Sessions, Information Form, Expression of Interest Submission Deadline.
e) About the Buyer/Specific Project: Information about the organization or individual issuing the EOI.

f) Limitations: The EOI must outline all legal implications from the outset to deter any legal action against the Buyer during and after the closing of the EOI process.

3. Distribution of Expression of Interest:

The distribution of the EOI depends on the size and type of the project. The Buyer may target specific Bidders or communities of interest that they have had limited previous contact with. The Buyer's contact lists and databases should form the foundation for the distribution list, which can be further edited and augmented through additional research. There are private organizations that compile lists of upcoming projects, where the Buyer can publish the EOI documents for better coverage.

4. Release the Expression of Interest:

The timing of the release of the Expression of Interest is determined by considering various aspects and ensuring it aligns with potential bidder respondents' schedules. Once the document is released, all inquiries must be tracked and followed up on. Frequently asked questions and any addendums should be posted online to keep all interested Bidders updated about the project.

5. Information Sessions: A good Buyer organization provides potential Bidders with an opportunity to learn more about the project. This may involve holding informal meetings or information sessions that outline the project and the requirements of the Expression of Interest. Depending on the project, Bidders may also be given the chance to visit the site and familiarize themselves with the location.

6. Expression of Interest Closes: The time provided for Bidders to respond to the Expression of Interest should be sufficient to allow them to assess the project, consult their board members (if required), and provide their responses.

The duration of this period may vary depending on the complexity of the project, ranging from a few days to a few weeks.

7. Expression of Interest Next Steps: The Expression of Interest document should clearly outline how and if the Bidders will be informed of the outcomes of the process. It is important to give all Bidders who have responded to the Expression of Interest an opportunity to find out about the outcomes. Additionally, it can be valuable to understand the reasons why some Bidders refrained from bidding, as this feedback can help improve the procurement process and attract a larger pool of qualified bidders.

Assuming the Buyer sent out the Expression of Interest to 5 shortlisted Bidders and received positive responses from 3 Bidders, the Buyer would proceed with discussions with the interested Bidders.

Step 7 – Inviting Bids: The Buyer or the professional organization hired to prepare the bids/tenders will now prepare a set of tenders, comprising the details elaborated in Table 1 above. These tenders will be issued to the shortlisted Bidders who have expressed interest in working with the Buyer.

At this stage, it is important to note the contents of the tender document and elaborate on certain important sections:

a) Notice Inviting Tender (NIT): A Notice Inviting Tender (NIT) is a formal procurement document issued by the Buyer, inviting Bidders to bid for the contract. This document is typically released after an Expression of Interest process, which helps the Buyer narrow down the potential Bidders. Bidders receive the NIT via email, online portals, or traditional letters. The NIT provides detailed information about the goods or services the Buyer needs to procure and specific considerations the Bidders are required to explore and provide for in order to be considered the most suitable.

The specific information included in the NIT can vary depending on the industry and Buyer's requirements. It provides more detailed information about the procurement needs and outlines the criteria that will be used to evaluate the Bidders. The NIT can be either a "closed tender" or an "open tender." In a closed tender, only the selected Bidders from the previous round (Expression of Interest) are invited to participate. In an open tender, the process starts directly with the NIT, allowing any interested Bidder to participate. It is important for both the Buyer and the Bidder to understand whether the tendering position is open or closed.

The following can be expected within a Notice Inviting Tender:

1. Scope of Works:

The Notice Inviting Tender should provide a detailed scope of works to reconfirm what was mentioned in the Expression of Interest. This includes information on timelines, expectations, concerns, and any technical aspects. For construction tenders, it may also include surveys, drawings, designs, pre-construction information, schedules, and supply chains.

2. Tender Specifics:

The Buyer should provide more information about themselves, along with instructions on how to submit the tender and details about the tender process. This includes critical information for the Bidders such as formats and the deadline date.

3. The Criteria:

The tender document should clearly outline the criteria and expectations of the Buyer. Bidders should thoroughly review and understand these criteria, highlighting where they can add value or provide unique selling points compared to other Bidders.

4. Assessment and Measurement of Criteria:

The Buyer should explain how they will evaluate and assess the tender responses based on the established criteria. Bidders should address these criteria in their responses and provide explanations, such as demonstrating value for money or outlining how they arrived at their tender value.

a) It is important for Bidders to consider the following aspects when responding to a Notice Inviting Tender:
   i. Review the submission method specified by the Buyer, whether it's uploading the submission to an online portal or adhering to specific page or word count limits.
   ii. Highlight key information that is important to the Bidder, such as critical elements of the specification or instructions. Take note of the submission deadline and seek clarification for any unclear aspects of the tender.
   iii. Assign specific areas of the response to different team members within the Bidder's organization, leveraging their expertise in relevant departments. Clearly communicate expectations, writing style, format, and deadlines to the team members. The person leading the tendering team should review and consolidate the responses, ensuring a cohesive and unified bid.
   iv. If there are any questions or uncertainties after reading the tender documents, it is recommended to seek clarification from the Buyer. This demonstrates the Bidder's interest, capability, and effective communication.
   v. Continuously refer to the criteria outlined in the tender and ensure that all aspects of the Buyer's requirements are covered. Buyers are interested in the technical solution and how the Bidder will meet their specific needs.
   vi. Showcase the Bidder's capabilities and key differentiators that align with the Buyer's requirements, distinguishing them from other Bidders.

vii. The bid writing process should involve frequent review and improvement, seeking feedback from team members to refine the content. Utilize the structure provided by the Buyer to address all elements of the tender.

viii. Before final submission, conduct a proofreading to check for spelling mistakes, punctuation, formatting, word counts, and terminology. Involve someone from the team who hasn't been directly involved in the content creation.

ix. After submission, gather the team to reflect on the bid, evaluate the process, and plan for future improvements. Identify areas for enhancement and consider lessons learned for future tender submissions.

b) Technical Specifications, Quality Expectations, and Drawings:

A specification is a document that describes in words what cannot be visualized or explained solely through drawings or models. It is crucial not only in construction but also in other industries such as aerospace, oil and gas, automobiles, and manufacturing. In construction, the specification covers various aspects, including:

- Site establishment
- Contract type
- Asset performance criteria
- Systems and product quality
- Applicable standards and their execution
- Specific products to be used

The type of specification can relate to the project or the procurement route, such as performance-based, prescriptive, or proprietary, depending on project requirements.

Specifications are essential during the design stage, as they form part of the contract documentation and play a key role in project fulfillment. Let's explore why specifications are crucial to the construction process:

a) Project Intent, Performance, and Construction Instructions:

Specifications provide clear instructions on the project's intent, performance requirements, and construction methods.

b) Reference to Quality and Standards:

Specifications can reference the quality and standards that should be applied in the project, ensuring compliance and consistency.

c) Clear Definition of Materials and Manufacturers' Products:

Specifications allow for the clear definition of materials and specific products to be used in the construction process.

d) Identification of Installation, Testing, and Handover Requirements:

Specifications identify the requirements for installation, testing, and handover of the completed project.

e) Classification for Handover and Asset Management:

Specifications support the classification of the project within the handover and asset management process, facilitating effective asset management and maintenance.

f) Information Overload Management:

By separating detailed information in the specification document, it helps avoid information overload on the drawings or models, making it easier to locate specific information.

g) Support for Project Costing:

Specifications support project costing by outlining not only the materials and products required but also the expected performance and workmanship.

h) Legal and Risk Management:

Specifications, along with drawings, form part of the contractual documents and help minimize project risks. They also provide support in case of legal disputes.

i) Interpretation of Buyer's Requirements:

Specifications support the interpretation of the Buyer's requirements, ensuring that the commissioned asset meets the Buyer's expectations.

j) Construction Phase Support:

Specifications are essential during the construction phase, providing guidance and information to the project team.

k) Time and Cost Savings:

By providing clear and concise information, specifications answer many construction-related questions, saving time and money for the project team, Buyer, and Contractor.

l) Continuous Improvement and Consistency:

After project completion, specifications contribute to continuous improvement by incorporating best practices and lessons learned. They enhance efficiency, provide quality assurance, and ensure project consistency.

m) Flexibility and Adaptability:

Specifications can be developed over time and adapted to suit specific project requirements, drawing on specialist knowledge when needed.

n) Utilization Beyond Design Phase:

Specifications are not limited to the design phase but serve as a living document for the complete project team throughout the construction phase.

o) Audit Trail and Handover Documents:

Specifications, along with any variations or value engineering, form part of the project's audit trail and crucial handover documents. They provide a basis for asset management, maintenance, and training.

Best practice dictates that specification writing should commence early in the project lifecycle. Early-stage specifications capture information from the Buyer's inputs, documenting their project objectives and performance requirements. Information gathered during discussions on complexes, entities, spaces, locations, elements, systems, and products contributes to the specification as it develops.

Globally, specifications can be categorized into two types: technical specifications and performance specifications.

• Technical Specifications: In this type, the Buyer clearly indicates the constituent elements of the product or service. The technical description can be presented schematically, through drawings, formulas, recipes with ingredients, or even test samples. The Bidder's task is to provide a product that fully corresponds to the technical description provided by the Buyer.

• Performance Specifications: Performance specifications provide the Bidder with information about the Buyer's expectations regarding the functions, performance, and anticipated results of the product or service. The Bidder has some flexibility in proposing items that meet the customer's expectations. Specifications can also be a combination of both technical and functional elements, depending on the specific project, product, or service being offered.

When considering practical examples, let's compare two requisitions:

1. Vague specification: I want a vehicle to drive from my home to office.
2. Clear specification: I want a white colour five-seater sedan car with 400 litres boot space which can operate on electricity.

Both orders involve cars, but they have different attributes specified. The clear specification in the second example allows the Buyer to measure the market against specific needs and achieve cost reduction by focusing on the specification without compromising fit, form, and function. The vague specification provides more flexibility but allows for the possibility of refining the specification as quotes are received.

Once the item is delivered, the specification serves as a basis for comparing the delivered item with the intended requirements. In the event of disputes or other commercial issues, the specification provides a formal method of identifying what the Buyer wanted and what was actually delivered.

A specification should be sufficiently detailed to ensure that the product or service meets the user's requirements. It should not be overly explicit (E.g. specifying only one brand of material) to prevent negotiation or discourage Buyers and suppliers from proposing alternative solutions that may offer better value for money. The preparation of a specification should involve close communication between the end user and the Buyer, and technical experts or potential Bidders may provide assistance if required. However, Bidder input should not result in a specification that favors a particular Bidder, as this could violate procurement policies of public and private organizations.

In general, brand names, trademarks, or specific origins should not be used in product specifications, unless the goods and services cannot be otherwise described precisely and intelligibly. In such cases, brand names should be accompanied by the words "or equivalent." Certain exceptions may be allowed, such as statutory duties, technical reasons, incompatibility or disproportionate costs, or for innovative purposes.

The **Bill of Quantities (BoQ)** has been used for over 300 years in the construction industry to price tenders based on designer drawings and determine the cost of a completed project before construction begins. It is a document that provides detailed descriptions of materials, workmanship, quality expectations, and quantities along with rates and amounts required for a construction project. The BOQ serves multiple functions throughout the project lifecycle:

1. Tendering Document: The BOQ serves as a tendering document, providing precise information for contractors to price the work with minimal effort.
2. Valuing Progress Payments: The BOQ is used to evaluate completed construction works for issuing interim payment certificates and progress payments.
3. Valuing Variations: The BOQ includes rates schedules that serve as a basis for evaluating variations or changes in the contract that affect the contract sum.
4. Project Costing: The BOQ is essential for project costing, estimating, and budgeting the overall cost of construction activities.
5. Database: The BOQ serves as a database of information, including materials, quantities, descriptions, and prices, which can be used for future estimations and similar construction projects.
6. Fee Calculation: The BOQ provides a basis for calculating consultants' fees by multiplying a certain percentage with the contract sum.
7. Asset Management: The BOQ contains information for asset management, such as life cycle costing studies, maintenance schedules, and insurance replacement costs.
8. Ordering of Materials: Contractors can use the BOQ to order and purchase materials by referring to the quantities and descriptions provided. (of course the quantities have to checked before ordering)

9. Elemental Cost Planning: The BOQ facilitates detailed cost planning by breaking down the project cost by elements of work.

10. Quality Analysis: The BOQ includes trade preamble clauses that support quality analysis and adherence to specified standards.

11. Quotations: The BOQ can be used to request quotations from sub-contractors and suppliers for various resources required in construction projects.

12. Fairest Competition for Tender: The BOQ ensures fair competition among tenderers as they price the work based on the same information.

13. Planning for Site Program: The BOQ helps in planning the site program, including resource programs, work breakdown structure, and progress monitoring.

14. Final Account: The BOQ is practical for final accounting, providing a basis for the final audit trail and agreement of all financial transactions related to the contract.

15. Cost Information and Control: The BOQ provides cost information for estimators, cost control during the contract, and ensuring work remains within budget.

The advantages of using the BOQ include lower estimating risks for contractors, fairer competition, detailed cost analysis, better control of variations, cost-effective management of subcontract work, and identification of potential problems during the measurement process.

While the usage of BOQs has declined for large projects, they still play a significant role in traditional contracts and other procurement routes that involve quantification and measurement processes. The BOQ's efficiency, accuracy, and ability to serve as a reference for changes and variations make it an important document in construction projects. Not using a BOQ can lead to problems such as contractors manipulating information, variations being difficult to value, and a higher risk of delays and cost overruns. Overall, the BOQ continues to be an essential document in construction projects, providing a structured and detailed approach to pricing, valuation, cost control, and project administration.

Program-expectations play a significant role in construction contracts. The program of works outlines the timeline and sequencing of construction activities and can be either a non-contractual reference point or a binding obligation for the parties involved. Including the program as a contract document has advantages and risks.

When the program is listed as a contract document, it becomes binding on both the Buyer and the Bidder/contractor. Any deviation from the program may constitute a breach of contract, entitling the aggrieved party to compensation for additional costs or delays. Buyers may benefit from including the program in the contract as it allows them greater control over the sequence of works and priority. Bidder/contractors also benefit from clear expectations and can plan their contributions accordingly.

However, there are pitfalls to including the program as a contract document, such as additional obligations for both parties, potential price increases, increased claims, delays to the commencement date, and delays during the construction period. If the program is binding, the Buyer must provide the necessary facilities and timely decisions to enable the Bidder/contractor to adhere to the program. Failure to do so may result in compensation claims from the Bidder/contractor for lost time and money.

A binding program can lead to an increase in claims and counter-claims between the parties, especially if there are multiple Bidders/contractors involved in the project. Both parties should clearly communicate their requirements and responsibilities regarding timing, documents, and access rights to mitigate this risk.

Bidder/contractors should consider the reduced flexibility and increased risk of claims associated with a binding program when pricing their bids.

They should clarify whether the program is a contract document early in the tender stage. Creating a contractually binding program adds complexity and may require involvement from techno-legal professionals to ensure consistency with the contract agreement.

The drafting and review process of the program may cause delays, as different parties need to align their inputs and requirements. Programs are typically live documents, subject to continuous updates based on on-site events. Amending a contractually binding program adds administrative burden and can further delay construction progress.

Standard forms of contracts provide guidance on dealing with programs, and further details can be found in the relevant sections of these contracts. Some of the common methods of preparing the programs are listed below:

a) Critical Path Analysis: Critical path analysis is a planning method that helps determine the most efficient path through a project by identifying tasks that are dependent on each other and must occur at the same time. It allows for prioritization and resource allocation based on the timeline of tasks.

b) Brainstorming: Brainstorming is a creative and collaborative technique used to gather input from the project team. It helps identify risks, concerns, and potential solutions that may not be immediately apparent. Brainstorming provides a holistic view of the project before formalizing the plan.

c) Work Breakdown Structure (WBS): The work breakdown structure breaks down a project into manageable tasks and provides a hierarchical structure. It starts with the project and breaks it down into phases, milestones, and tasks. This method helps understand the scope of the project and allocate resources, schedule, and budget accordingly.

d) Gantt Chart: The Gantt chart is a visual representation of a project schedule that shows tasks, dependencies, and timelines. It allows project managers to track progress, identify overlaps or delays, and manage resources effectively. Gantt charts are widely used in project management software and provide a flexible and comprehensive overview of the project.

e) Program Evaluation and Review Technique (PERT): PERT is a planning method that helps estimate the time required for a project. It breaks down tasks, establishes task dependencies, and assigns time estimates for each task. By calculating the expected time and variance for each task, PERT provides a more accurate estimation of the overall project timeline, considering the uncertainties and dependencies involved.

Programs, in general, describe the sequence of tasks to be carried out in order to complete a project or its specific parts on time. They provide a roadmap for project execution and serve as a reference for project management and control throughout the project lifecycle.

Step 8 – Techno Commercial Negotiations:

During the negotiation stage, it is crucial to focus not only on the commercial aspects such as pricing but also on other relevant points related to the scope of work and project requirements. Prioritizing these discussions helps ensure a comprehensive understanding of the project and avoids overlooking critical details.

Here are some key points to consider during techno commercial negotiations:

1. Scope Clarification: Discuss and clarify all aspects of the scope of work, including logistics, infrastructure requirements, and dependencies. Address any potential challenges or specific needs that may impact the project's execution.

2. Timeline and Milestones: Engage in detailed discussions regarding the expected timeline for project completion. Define interim milestones and points of reference to track progress and ensure timely delivery. This helps align the contractor's timeline with the Buyer's requirements.

3. Statutory Compliance and Taxation: Clarify the responsibilities and obligations related to statutory compliances, permits, licenses, and taxation requirements. Ensure both parties have a clear understanding of the legal and regulatory aspects relevant to the project and who is responsible for these

4. Commercial Terms: Once all other aspects are addressed, the negotiation can move on to the rates, amounts, and other commercial aspects. Discuss payment schedules, any necessary advances, and the final amount for the scope of work. This includes considering the overall financial terms and conditions of the contract.

5. Final Discussions and Agreement: Conduct detailed negotiations with all shortlisted Bidders and hold a final round of discussions with the potential Bidder who is considered the best fit for the contract. Review the entire scope, terms and conditions, exclusions, and the final amount with the selected Bidder.

6. Draft Contract Agreement: After the discussions and alignment of all terms, it is recommended to share a draft purchase order or contract agreement with the potential Bidder. This allows them to review and confirm that the draft accurately reflects the discussions and agreements reached thus far.

7. Execution of Contract Agreement: Once the potential Bidder, now referred to as the contractor, agrees to the draft contract agreement, the Buyer and the contractor proceed to execute a detailed contract agreement. Both parties sign off on the agreement, indicating their acceptance and commitment to its terms and conditions.

8. Contract Registration: Depending on the country of operation, there may be a requirement to register the contract agreement with the appropriate government authorities by paying a certain amount of duty. This step provides evidence of the existence of the agreement in case of any future disputes.

The process of contract execution can now be facilitated digitally in many countries, offering convenience and flexibility to all parties involved.

However, specific digital contract execution processes and platforms should be explored based on the country's legal and regulatory requirements.

By following these steps, techno commercial negotiations can be conducted comprehensively, ensuring that all aspects of the project are addressed and the contract agreement reflects the mutual understanding and expectations of both the Buyer and the contractor.

Step 9 - Kick-off Meeting and Contract Execution

After the contract agreement is finalized and signed by both the Buyer and the contractor, it is important to conduct a formal kick-off meeting. The kick-off meeting brings together key stakeholders and project team members to ensure a common understanding of the project scope, objectives, timelines, and responsibilities. The meeting provides an opportunity to discuss the project plan, communication channels, reporting mechanisms, and any specific requirements or concerns.

During the kick-off meeting, the following points should be addressed:

1. Introductions: Allow all attendees to introduce themselves, including representatives from the Buyer, the contractor, and any other relevant parties.
2. Project Overview: Provide an overview of the project, including its objectives, scope, deliverables, and desired outcomes. Clarify any specific project requirements or expectations.
3. Roles and Responsibilities: Clearly define the roles and responsibilities of each project team member, including the Buyer, the contractor, consultants, and any other involved parties. Ensure everyone understands their respective tasks and areas of accountability.
4. Communication Plan: Establish an effective communication plan that outlines how project-related information will be shared, who the key points of contact are, and the preferred communication channels (e.g., meetings, emails, project management software).

5. Project Schedule and Milestones: Review the project schedule, including key milestones and deliverables. Discuss any critical dates, dependencies, or potential challenges that need to be addressed.

6. Risk Management: Identify potential risks and discuss strategies for mitigating them. Encourage open communication and collaboration to proactively address any project risks or issues that may arise.

7. Quality Assurance: Discuss the quality standards and expectations for the project. Establish protocols for quality control, inspections, and testing procedures to ensure that project deliverables meet the required standards.

8. Health and Safety: Emphasize the importance of health and safety on the project site. Discuss safety protocols, emergency procedures, and any specific requirements or regulations that need to be followed.

9. Contractual Obligations: Review the terms and conditions of the contract agreement, including payment terms, warranties, dispute resolution mechanisms, and any specific contractual obligations that need to be fulfilled.

10. Next Steps: Summarize the key points discussed during the meeting and outline the next steps and action items. Assign responsibilities and establish timelines for specific tasks.

It is essential to document the discussions, decisions, and action items from the kick-off meeting in meeting minutes or a formal project initiation document. This serves as a reference for all stakeholders and helps ensure that everyone is aligned and accountable throughout the project.

By conducting a thorough kick-off meeting and effectively executing the contract, the project can start on a strong foundation, with clear expectations, effective communication channels, and a shared understanding of the project's objectives and requirements.

Step 10 – Contract Administration:

Contract administration is a continuous process that spans the duration of the contract. It involves managing and overseeing the execution of the contract, ensuring compliance with contractual obligations, monitoring progress, and addressing any issues or changes that may arise.

Key aspects of contract administration include:

1. Payment and Invoicing: Ensure that payments are made according to the agreed-upon terms and schedule. Review and verify invoices submitted by the contractor, and process them in a timely manner.
2. Change Management: Implement a formal change management process to address any changes to the project scope, specifications, schedule, or budget. Evaluate change requests, assess their impact, and obtain necessary approvals before implementing changes.
3. Progress Monitoring: Regularly monitor the progress of the project against the planned schedule and milestones. Identify any delays, issues, or deviations from the original plan and take appropriate actions to mitigate risks and keep the project on track.
4. Documentation Management: Maintain a comprehensive record of all project-related documents, including contracts, correspondence, minutes of meetings, change orders, and other relevant documentation. Ensure proper organization, version control, and accessibility of these documents.
5. Communication and Collaboration: Foster effective communication and collaboration among all stakeholders involved in the project. Establish regular project meetings, provide progress updates, and address any concerns or queries promptly.
6. Quality Control: Implement quality control measures to ensure that project deliverables meet the required standards and specifications. Conduct inspections, audits, and testing as necessary to verify compliance with quality requirements.
7. Dispute Resolution: Establish a mechanism for resolving disputes that may arise during the contract execution. Follow the agreed-upon dispute resolution procedures, such as negotiation, mediation, or arbitration, to address conflicts and reach mutually acceptable resolutions.

8. Contract Closeout: As the project nears completion, initiate the contract closeout process. Ensure that all contractual obligations have been fulfilled, conduct a final inspection or acceptance process, and facilitate the final payment and release of any remaining contract securities.

By effectively administering the contract, stakeholders can ensure that the project is executed in accordance with the agreed terms, mitigate risks, maintain project control, and foster successful project outcomes. Regular monitoring, documentation, and communication are vital for successful contract administration.

Step 11 – Defects Liability Period:

In construction contracts, there is typically a defects liability period specified in the contract. This period usually ranges from 12 to 24 months starting from the date of issuing the taking over certificate by the Buyer. During this period, the Buyer has the opportunity to identify and notify the contractor of any defects or issues that arise in the project.

The defects liability period serves as a warranty period where the contractor is responsible for rectifying any defects in materials, workmanship, or non-compliance with specifications. The Buyer should inspect and report any defects promptly to the contractor during this period.

The process during the defects liability period includes:

1. Defect Notification: The Buyer should notify the contractor in writing about any defects observed during the defects liability period. The notification should clearly describe the nature and location of the defects.
2. Contractor's Obligations: Upon receiving the defect notification, the contractor is obligated to inspect, investigate, and rectify the

reported defects within a reasonable timeframe as specified in the contract.

3. Rectification of Defects: The contractor should take necessary actions to repair or replace any defective work, materials, or components to meet the required standards and specifications.

4. Verification and Acceptance: Once the contractor has rectified the reported defects, the Buyer should verify the effectiveness of the rectification works. If the rectification is satisfactory, the Buyer issues a certificate of making good defects or similar document to acknowledge the completion of the defect rectification.

5. Release of Retention: In construction contracts, a retention amount is often withheld from the contractor's payments during the defects liability period. Upon successful rectification and acceptance of all defects, the Buyer releases the retained amount to the contractor.

It is important to adhere to the procedures and timelines outlined in the contract regarding defect notifications, rectifications, and acceptance. Clear communication between the Buyer and the contractor is essential to ensure that all defects are appropriately addressed and resolved within the defects liability period.

Step 12 – Closure of the Contract:

The closure of the contract marks the final stage of the project, indicating the successful completion of the contractual obligations by both parties. It involves formalizing the completion of the project and concluding all contractual matters.

The process for the closure of the contract includes:

1. Performance Certificate: Once the defects liability period has expired, and all defects have been rectified to the satisfaction of the Buyer, the Buyer issues a performance certificate to the contractor. The performance certificate acknowledges that the contractor has fulfilled their obligations under the contract.

2. Final Payments: With the issuance of the performance certificate, any outstanding payments or adjustments are finalized. The Buyer releases the final payment to the contractor, including the release of any remaining contract securities, such as performance bonds or guarantees. Similar to the Performance Certificate, the Contractor may also be expected to provide a "No Claims Certificate" to the Employer stating that, upon receipt of the final payment as mentioned in the No Claims Certificate, there will not be any further claims from the Contractor to the Employer for the specific contract.

3. Document Retention: Both the Buyer and the contractor should retain copies of all relevant project documents, including contracts, drawings, specifications, reports, and correspondences. These documents may need to be preserved for a specified period as required by legal or regulatory obligations.

4. Lessons Learned: It is beneficial for both the Buyer and the contractor to conduct a project review or lessons learned session. This provides an opportunity to reflect on the project's successes, challenges, and areas for improvement. The insights gained can be used to enhance future project management practices.

5. Feedback and Evaluation: The Buyer may provide feedback to the contractor regarding their performance, adherence to quality standards, and overall satisfaction with the project outcome. This feedback can be valuable for the contractor's continuous improvement and future reference.

6. The formal closure of the contract signifies the end of the contractual relationship between the Buyer and the contractor. However, maintaining a positive professional relationship and open communication can pave the way for potential future collaborations.

Please note that the specific steps and processes may vary depending on the contract terms, project requirements, and applicable laws and regulations in the relevant jurisdiction.

In this chapter, we have covered the final steps of the tendering process, including the kick-off meeting, contract administration, defects liability period, and closure of the contract. The kick-off meeting serves as an important event to bring together all stakeholders and establish clear communication channels and expectations. Contract administration involves managing the contractual obligations, timelines, payments, and compliance throughout the duration of the contract.

The defects liability period allows the Buyer to notify the contractor of any defects in the delivered work, which the contractor is obligated to rectify. Finally, the closure of the contract is marked by the issuance of a performance certificate by the Buyer and a No Claims Certificate by the Contractor, signaling the successful completion of the project and the release of any retained payments or securities.

It is emphasized that maintaining a positive working relationship and effective communication between the parties is crucial during the entire contract process.

Feedback and lessons learned should be shared for future improvement. Additionally, the importance of adhering to legal and statutory requirements, as well as retaining necessary contract documents, is highlighted.

The chapter concludes by reiterating the key takeaways, such as the importance of assessing the contractor and the Buyer, understanding the Buyer's capability, and following the recommended steps in the tendering process.

It is mentioned that while the focus has been on traditional contracting for small and medium-sized organizations, there are other approaches for complex contracts that involve early contractor involvement in design stages.

The next chapter will delve into the major terms and clauses typically found in a contract agreement, providing further insights into contract management and implementation.

Call to action:

The reader is requested to review the processes followed in their organizations or projects and compare with all the steps mentioned above. In case of any major deviations to above, they can write or discuss about that on www.prasamviidah.com or manish.mohandas@outlook.com

CHAPTER 2:

MAJOR TERMS OF ANY AGREEMENT

Now that you are fully aware of the vital steps to be considered before signing a contract and the requirements that have to be followed after execution of the Contract Agreement, let us delve into the next most important and insightful section, where we will learn the crucial conditions that any agreement must have and the elements that form part of any contract.

For any contract agreement to be watertight and to safeguard the interests of all parties involved, it is imperative to include all foreseeable aspects and scenarios that may arise during the tenure of the contract.

Despite your best efforts, there can be situations where you may have to confront unforeseen obstacles that may not have been present while signing the contract. However, a good amount of thought at the initial stage of the contract agreement will help both parties involved anticipate all possible scenarios and address them within the contract agreement in a way that protects their interests.

Drafting a contract taking into account all foreseeable scenarios help in maintaining transparency in negotiations in the event of any disputes that may arise in the future. This also helps in reducing disputes and maintain healthy business relationships.

Here, we will split our discussions into 2 parts as below:

Part 1 – Before signing the Contract Agreement

Prior to signing the contract agreement, the Buyer and the seller need to discuss and clarify all the requirements from both sides. From the Buyer's perspective, it is essential to define specific expectations such as instructions to bidders, quality requirements, safety requirements, technical specifications, timelines, etc. For example, in our specific case of Bob's dream house, Bob needs to clarify his specific requirement to his potential Contractor in the form of instructions to bidders. He should provide the size of his house through relevant drawings and specify the materials and workmanship standards he would like the contractor to adhere to. Additionally, other logistics-related plans should also be discussed. Let us now understand the importance of each of these elements that need to be clarified before the execution of the contract agreement.

Instruction to Bidders: This is a crucial section of any contract agreement. While the bidder is competing to secure the contract, there will be expenses incurred by the bidder. For instance, the bidder will need to visit the location where Bob wants his house to be constructed. The expenses incurred during such visits must be covered by the bidder.

This aspect needs to be explicitly clarified in the Instructions to Bidders. Since multiple bidders are vying for the contract to construct Bob's dream house, it should be made clear that Bob, as the buyer, will not reimburse any bidders for expenses incurred prior to executing the contract agreement. These expenses are considered part of the business development costs for the respective bidding companies.

Here's another situation: if Bob decides not to proceed with the construction of his dream house after receiving the bids, he, as the buyer, is not obligated to make any payments to the bidding organizations.

However, this should be explicitly stated in the Instructions to Bidders so that bidders are aware of the risks associated with bidding for Bob's dream house construction project.

Consider a situation where arithmetic errors occur in the submitted bids. In such a case, Bob, as the buyer, or any of his representatives, would rectify the arithmetic error independently and make a decision based on the corrected sums provided by the bidder. These aspects must be specifically outlined in the "Instruction to Bidders" document.

Another clarification that may be included in the Instruction to Bidders document is that the buyer can select any bidder based on criteria that aligns with the buyer's requirements. In this context, Bob, as the buyer, is not obligated to provide any explanation for rejecting bids. This is an essential condition that should be specified in the Instruction to Bidders document.

Depending on the industry in which the agreement is being implemented, various other requirements may also be explicitly stated in the Instruction to Bidders document.

This document becomes vital before executing the contract agreement as it establishes the framework under which bidders are expected to submit bids for the subject contract.

In short, **Instructions to Bidders** is a document that provides Bidders with the information needed to prepare their technical and financial Bids. The following General Instructions for Bidders shall apply to all tenders:

MAJOR TERMS OF ANY AGREEMENT

1. DEFINITIONS

The following terms will have the following meanings:

a) "Tender" will mean any invitation to Bidders to provide in writing an Offer to supply goods, services, and/or works to the Buyer which is issued in any form (i.e., Request for quotation, Invitation to Bid, or Request for Proposal) by the Buyer.

b) "Offer" will mean a proposal, quotation, offer, or bid submitted in writing to the Buyer in response to a Tender.

c) "Bidder" will mean a subject (i.e., individual, company, organization, or other entity) submitting an Offer in response to a Tender.

d) "Contract" will mean any written agreement concluded between the Buyer and the selected Bidder as a result of the Offer being accepted by the Buyer.

e) "In writing" or "written" will mean by letter, fax, or any standard electronic communication means (i.e., E-mail). In some cases, certain technologies like WhatsApp also may be treated as an acceptable form of communication.

2. SUBMISSION OF THE OFFER

a) Form of submission of Offers: Detailed instructions for the submission of Offers are defined in each Tender. Failure to observe such instructions may lead to rejection of the Offer.

b) Costs of submission: The Bidder shall bear all costs associated with preparing and submitting an Offer. The Buyer will in no case be responsible or liable for those costs, regardless of the conduct or outcome of the Tender.

c) Language of submissions: Offers and any related communications shall be submitted in English unless specified otherwise in the Tender. In any event, if documents are submitted in English and another language, the English version of the text shall prevail. In some regions, the local language may prevail.

d) Closing Date: The Buyer must receive Offers by the closing date and time specified in the Tender. Offers received after this date and time MAY NOT BE CONSIDERED. They may be returned unopened to the concerned Bidder(s) or, in case of submissions by electronic communications means, will be deleted. The Buyer may in some cases extend the deadline upon request from the Bidders.

e) Withdrawal or modification of Offers: Bidders may withdraw, replace, or modify their Offer until the closing date for the submission of Offers, provided that this is done in writing. Any modification or replacement of an Offer must be done in the same format as defined in the Tender. Bidders shall not be permitted to alter their Offers after the expiry of the deadline for the submission of Offers.

f) Clarifications: Bidders may request additional information or clarifications during the Tender process with respect to the requirements set out in the Tender documents. Any clarifications required by a Bidder must be requested in writing by email to the specified email address. Such requests must be submitted before the closing date for the submission of Offers, and in any case, no later than the deadline for seeking clarifications specified in the Tender to allow proper consideration and a reply. The Buyer will provide the response to a request for clarifications submitted by any Bidder simultaneously in writing to all known potential Bidders without necessarily disclosing the source of the query. The Buyer reserves the right to modify the documents through a Tender Clarification communicated to all bidders. In the event of an amendment to the Tender documents, the Buyer reserves the right to extend the closing date for the submission of Offers. No information shall be provided to any Bidders regarding the probability of acceptance of an Offer.

g) Validity of an Offer: For major tender, an Offer shall remain valid for acceptance for a period of at least 90 days from the closing date indicated in the Tender unless otherwise stated.

h) Due diligence: The Bidders must fully familiarize themselves with all instructions, forms, contract conditions, terms, and specifications in the Tender documents. Bidders must thoroughly review and analyze all maps, locations, drawings, technical specifications, schedules, and other instructions provided. Neglecting to do so will be at the bidder's own risk and accountability, and it will not grant them the authority to alter or retract their offer after the specified deadline.

i) No obligation to contract: The issuance of a Tender, whether public or not, does not commit the Buyer to award a Contract due to the Tender process. The Buyer may not pay any costs incurred by a Bidder in preparing or submitting an Offer. Any Offer submitted will be regarded as an Offer made by the Bidder and not as an acceptance by the Bidder of an Offer made by the buyer.

j) Cancellation of Tender: The Buyer may reserve the right to cancel a Tender at any stage of the procurement process before the final notice of award of a Contract. In this case, all Bidders shall be informed thereof.

k) Confidentiality: All offers from bidders and communications with the Bidders relating to such Offers will be kept strictly confidential by the Buyer before, during, and after the award. All Tender documentation is the property of the Buyer; no part thereof, or any information contained therein, may be published, used, or copied without the prior written consent of the Buyer.

l) Use of former Buyer employees in the preparation of Offers: As a good business practice, a Bidder must not be associated, or must not have been associated in the past, with a person who contributes to, or participates in, any process relating to the preparation of an Offer and/or in the procurement process, if that person:

i. At any time during the 12 months immediately preceding the date of issuance of the Tender has represented the Buyer; or

ii. At any time during the 24 months immediately preceding the date of issuance of the Tender was personally involved, directly or indirectly, in the definition of the requirements, project or activity to which the Tender relates. In addition to any other remedies available to it, the Buyer may, at its sole discretion, immediately reject any Offer submitted by a Bidder that, in the Buyer's sole opinion, has been found to be associated with a person as described above.

m) Corrupt practices: The Bidders shall not at any time in the course of the procurement process, be it before or after the award of the Contract, grant, promise or offer any direct or indirect benefit, whether of financial or other nature, to any official, agent, servant or employee of, or any person otherwise engaged by, the Buyer. In addition to any other remedies available to it, the Buyer may, at its sole discretion, immediately reject any Offer submitted by a Bidder that, in the Buyer's sole opinion, has engaged in corrupt practices.

n) Conflict of Interest: A Bidder must ensure that its employees, officers, advisers, agents, or subcontractors do not place themselves in a position that may give rise to an actual, potential, or apparent conflict of interest between the interests of the Buyer and the Bidder's interests during the procurement process. Conflict of interest means having an interest, whether personal, financial, or otherwise, which interferes or may be perceived as interfering with the ability of the Bidder to submit a fair and objective Offer or the ability of the Buyer to evaluate Offers fairly and objectively. In addition to any other remedies available, the Buyer may, at its sole discretion, immediately reject any Offer submitted by a Bidder that, in the Buyer's sole opinion, has an actual, potential, or apparent conflict of interest.

o) Collusion Bidding and Other Unethical Conduct: Bidders and their employees, officers, advisers, agents, or sub-contractors must not engage in any collusive bidding or other anticompetitive conduct, or any other similar conduct, in relation to:

i. The preparation or submission of Offers.

ii. The clarification of Offers.

iii. The conduct and content of negotiations, including final Contract negotiations, with respect to the Tender, the procurement process, or any other process being conducted by the Buyer.

In addition to any other remedies available to it, the Buyer may, at its sole discretion, immediately reject any Offer submitted by a Bidder that, in the Buyer's sole opinion, has engaged in any collusive bidding, other anti-competitive conduct or any other similar conduct with any other Bidder, person or entity in relation to the preparation or submission of Offers, or any other procurement process being conducted by the Buyer. Bidder can participate in the Tender individually or as a joint venture or consortium member. However, participation in both capacities may not be allowed and will disqualify all Offers submitted with the Bidder's participation. Offers submitted by a joint venture or consortium shall provide the full name and address of all partners and/or Bidders.

p) Undue advantage: Any Offers that, in the sole opinion of the Buyer, have been prepared with the assistance of current or former officials, agents, servants or employees of, or persons otherwise engaged by the Buyer in violation of confidentiality obligations, or by using information not otherwise available to other Bidders, or which would provide an undue advantage in the procurement process, may be excluded from further consideration. Depending on the extent of the breach, Bidders may be suspended from temporarily dealing with the Buyer or classified as ineligible and therefore excluded from participation to further Buyer Tenders.

q) Ineligibility of blacklisted Bidders: The Buyer reserves the right to declare a bidder ineligible to participate in a Tender. Buyer has the authority to reject a Bidder that has been debarred, sanctioned, or otherwise declared ineligible.

3. SUPPLIER REGISTRATION PROCEDURE

Pre-Requisites for Eligibility: As part of the supplier registration application, all Bidders may be required to declare (both for parent and/or subsidiary entities, as applicable) that the company:

a) Is not a company or associated with a company or individual under procurement prohibition by the Buyer,

b) Is not currently blacklisted by the Buyer,

c) Is not under formal investigation, nor has been blacklisted within the preceding three (3) years by any national authority for engaging or having engaged in illegal practices, including but not limited to corruption, fraud, coercion, collusion, obstruction, or any other unethical practice,

d) Has not declared bankruptcy, is not involved in bankruptcy or receivership proceedings, and there is no judgment or pending legal action against them that could impair their operations in the foreseeable future,

e) Does not employ, or anticipate employing, any person(s) who is, or has been a Buyer staff member within the last year if said Buyer staff member has or had prior professional dealings with the Bidder in his/her capacity as Buyer staff member within the last three years of service,

f) Undertakes not to engage in illegal practices (including but not limited to corruption, fraud, or any other unethical practice), with the Buyer or any other party and to conduct business in a manner that averts any financial, operational, reputational or other undue risk to the Buyer.

Changes in Bidder's Situation: If a Bidder's situation changes about any of the statements listed above after being included in the Supplier

Register, the Bidder shall immediately inform the Buyer thereof. Non-compliance with this requirement may automatically render the Bidder ineligible.

4. EVALUATION OF THE OFFER

a) Clarifications: To assist in the examination, evaluation, and comparison of Offers, the Buyer may, at its discretion, ask a Bidder for clarification about the content of its Offer. The request for clarification and the response shall be made in writing, and no change in price or substance of the Offer shall be sought, offered, or accepted.

b) Errors: The Buyer will usually correct arithmetical errors discovered during an Offer's examination. If the correction will affect the total price of an Offer, the Bidder(s) will be informed of such correction. If there is a discrepancy between words and figures, the amount in words will usually prevail. The Offer may be rejected if the Bidder does not accept the correction of arithmetical errors.

c) Information: The evaluation of an Offer will be conducted based on all the information provided in the documentation submitted in response to the Tender, including possible clarifications requested by the Buyer. In addition, a Bidder may be requested to provide evidence of its technical qualifications and financial soundness. The Buyer may reserve the right to independently verify such information.

d) Independent Tenders and Offers: Each Offer from a Bidder will be considered separately and independently from other Offers of the same Bidder submitted in response to other Tenders. Bidders shall submit a complete Offer for each Tender in which they wish to participate. References to previous or ongoing Offers may not be considered. The award of a previous Contract with the Buyer may not be considered a preference or guarantee for the award of future Contracts with respect to Tenders on the same subject.

e) Evaluation Criteria: The selection methods applied to evaluate the Offers and to determine the award of a Contract, including evaluation criteria, are defined in each Tender. This may or may not be shared with the Bidders for any tenders issued by private organizations.

5. AWARD AND CONTRACT

a) Acceptance of the Contract and Price Negotiations: Upon acceptance of an Offer by the Buyer and award of a Contract, the selected Bidder shall be prepared to sign the Contract and to perform the work/services or provide the goods as described in the accepted Offer. Refusal or reservations to sign a Contract awarded by the Buyer may lead to the exclusion of the Bidder from further Buyer Tenders, without prejudice to any other remedies that the Buyer may use as a consequence of such refusal or reservations. The Buyer reserves the right to conduct price negotiations until a final agreement is reached. Refusal to sign the contract by a Bidder may result in the Bidder losing any deposit (e.g. Earnest Money Deposit) which the Bidder may have submitted along with the Tender.

b) Written Contract: Generally, a contractual relationship with the Buyer is established only after a final written Contract document is signed by a duly authorized official of the Buyer and of the selected Bidder. Any activity undertaken or expenses incurred before an actual Contract is signed shall be borne by the Bidder. An advance notice (also known as a Letter of Intent) or award information is NOT to be considered a Contract.

c) Buyer's General Terms and Conditions of Contract: The final Contract will include the Buyer's General Terms and Conditions for the Purchase of Services or the Buyer's General Terms and Conditions for the Purchase of Goods, as applicable. The Bidder shall explicitly state in the submission of its Offer that such General Terms and Conditions are read, understood, and accepted. Failure to indicate acceptance of the General Terms and Conditions may lead to rejection of an Offer.

d) Information to unsuccessful Bidders: Unsuccessful Bidders shall be informed of the procurement process's outcome after the contract's conclusion with the selected Bidder.

6. INQUIRIES AND PROTEST PROCEDURES –

The provisions below establish the procedures available to Bidders to address concerns concerning a procurement process. Such protests are usually available only in the case of government tenders or tenders issued by private organizations that use public funds. These procedures are without prejudice to the immunity of the Buyer from the legal process:

a) "Inquiry" shall mean a written question from the Bidder concerning his/her Offer with respect to the evaluation procedure other than a clarification concerning the content of the Tender documents.

b) "Protest" shall mean a challenge of the award decision put forward by a Bidder.

c) The Buyer shall receive inquiries from unsuccessful Bidders with respect to Tender procedures. The Buyer shall ensure that a written acknowledgment of an inquiry has been issued within a specified number of working days. Information provided by the Buyer in response to an inquiry shall be limited to the reasons for the failure of the Bidder's Offer and the relevant information on the evaluation process. Information regarding the offers made by other bidders in the relevant procurement process shall not be disclosed to the bidders.

d) If, following the conclusion of the process, the Bidder remains dissatisfied, the Bidder may submit a formal Protest to the Buyer. A Protest shall be in writing and consist of a detailed statement of all factual and legal grounds for the Protest, a detailed explanation of how the Bidder considers that it was prejudiced, and any evidence or documentation supporting the Protest.

e) Upon receipt of a written Protest, the Buyer shall issue a written acknowledgment. The Buyer may decide to recommend an appropriate process for the resolution of the Protest

Technical specifications:

Although Chapter 1 provides extensive explanations of this particular aspect, it is important to briefly revisit it here once more. Any contractor can build the works only if they know the contract's specific requirements. In the case of our example of Bob's dream house, what specific information would Bob need to share with the potential bidders to ensure the successful construction of his house?

• The house in terms of square footage or number of bedrooms, the size of the bedrooms, the size of the living room, the height of the rooms, the number of floors that he prefers his house to have, etc.

• The quality of materials used in the house and the type of materials. For example, would Bob prefer his dream house to be constructed using wood, metal, concrete, or a combination of these? Would Bob prefer to use natural stones such as granite or marble? Or would he rather prefer to use artificial products such as tiles? Would Bob like to have his dream house painted with a specific type of paint, or would he like to have his house with a raw finish?

• When would Bob like to have his house completed and ready for use? Would Bob like to have his house completed in 12 months? What would happen if the house is not completed within 12 months? Would Bob have to pay the rental charges for some arrangement? Or is there a larger impact if the house is not constructed within the agreed timelines? If the house has two floors, but Bob would like the first floor to be constructed first, would he be staying there while the construction is going on the second floor? Is this acceptable by local government standards?

- Are there any restrictions on working hours in the location where Bob's dream house is being constructed? For instance, working during the night is likely to be restricted in a residential area. Additionally, there may be restrictions on working in the afternoon for a few hours in certain areas. It is crucial to inform potential bidders about these limitations in advance before inviting bids. This ensures that the bidders can accurately price their bids based on this information.

- Are there any traffic-related limitations or regulations affecting the location where Bob's envisioned house is being built? For instance, does the area have one-way streets during certain hours? Is it necessary for large vehicles to access the site? Are there any restrictions regarding the dimensions of vehicles that can reach the location? Additionally, are there any small bridges along the route with weight limits, posing potential constraints?

- Do the weather conditions in the area impose any limitations? For instance, in areas with heavy snowfall, the bidder might have constraints on working during specific times of the year. Similarly, in areas with high rainfall, there may be limitations on the bidder's ability to work during certain periods of the year.

The above-mentioned are a few details that must be communicated to the prospective bidders before they submit their proposals. Ensuring that the bids received meet the necessary technical and commercial criteria is imperative.

Bob is providing this information to ensure that the chosen bidder for his house construction comprehends the full scope of the project and is capable of completing it according to Bob's specifications and within the expected timeframe.

Suppose the aforementioned information is not accurately provided. In that case, it is likely that the bidder could misjudge the project, leading to either project abandonment or the need for additional funding and time to complete it both of which are unfavorable for Bob.

In line with the previously examined instances regarding Bob's vision for his dream house, any project, regardless of its nature, necessitates the identification and documentation of specific requirements. By doing so, it becomes imperative for potential bidders to understand the project at hand comprehensively. Thus, it is paramount that the buyer or their representatives diligently compile and incorporate all the important prerequisites in the bid or tender. This is to facilitate a thorough comprehension of the project by the bidders. A list of such examples, which are usually used for construction projects, are provided at www.prasamviidah.com.

Conditions of Contract

It is important for Bob to specify other relevant conditions of the contract. Various contract forms can be used, which are discussed in detail in subsequent chapters. It is important to check that all important conditions have been incorporated into the tender documents. Of course, these conditions could undergo some changes based on the technical and commercial discussions and negotiations that would surface after Bob receives bids from the bidders. The changes that have been mutually agreed between Bob and the selected bidder would eventually form part of the contract agreement.

The abovementioned information is an indicative list that must be provided along with any tender documents. These requirements have to be discussed and concluded by the Buyer's organization, taking into account all requirements that are required to be satisfied.

Once the requirements have been passed on to the bidders, a series of techno-commercial negotiations would follow. After completion of such techno-commercial negotiations, the Bidder would enter into a detailed contract agreement. Let us now move on to the next segment of the chapter to explore the important conditions (boilerplate conditions) that must be captured in the contract agreement apart from other conditions that may be agreed upon.

Part 2 – Within the Contract Agreement

The components of a typical contract agreement will be discussed in detail in Chapter 4. Certain contract conditions, known as boilerplate conditions, must be carefully considered and included to avoid negative consequences for both parties. Although all contract conditions are significant in some manner, neglecting these important conditions would have repercussions on both parties. The term "boilerplate" originated in the 1890s, when text plates for advertisements or syndicated columns were created in steel and then distributed to newspapers across the United States for printing. They were called boilerplates because they resembled the thick, tough steel sheets used to build steam boilers. Subsequently, the term 'boilerplate' came to denote the clauses that were part and parcel of each agreement without any changes because they were set and standardized. Sometimes they are categorized into miscellaneous provisions of the contract. They are rarely negotiated between the parties and are assumed to denote only the existing provisions in the earlier contract. However, there is no set definition of 'boilerplate clause'; it is used to denote a set of common clauses in all contracts. For some contracts in particular industries like construction, contracts have a determined set of boilerplate clauses, which may not be found in other contracts. Hence, there is no firm opinion as to whether or not the boilerplate clauses are restricted to a few clauses. Some opinions include the clauses at the beginning of the agreement in the boilerplate clauses. In contrast, most of the opinion includes only the clauses at the end of the agreement in the boilerplate clauses.

Why are boilerplate clauses necessary?

Boilerplate clauses deal with an agreement's interpretation, validity, and enforcement. As such, they significantly impact the agreement and can find themselves as the cause of litigation. Most parties don't sufficiently consider the impact of their boilerplate clauses or even the benefits they may bring. The purpose of boilerplate clauses is to protect the interests of all parties that sign the contract. In practice, some may favor one party over the other, so you need to specify them.

Contracts are entered between the parties so that both parties duly comply with the terms and conditions mentioned in the agreement. However, there can be certain situations where a dispute or difference may arise between them in the future. That is when Boilerplate-clauses come into play. After discussing the commercials between the parties, the Boilerplate clauses are generally placed at the end of the agreement. Boilerplate clauses give direction to the parties to handle a situation that can arise in the future.

These clauses address a range of things, such as the consequences that may arise if a document is declared unenforceable, how disputes will be resolved, which laws govern the contract, and more.

Does a Contract really need Boilerplate clauses?

There's no legal requirement to include boilerplate clauses in commercial contracts. Contracts can operate perfectly well without them. The necessity of a boilerplate clause is determined by the type of contract and the action that will take place as part of the contract. You have to ensure that the wording in the clause is appropriate. Small changes in the wording of standard boilerplate clauses can make a dramatic difference to the legal effect of the contract, as you can see from the list of examples below. And rarely will every boilerplate clause be required for a commercial or business contract. Often it won't make sense to include all of them. In some cases, boilerplate clauses remove legal rights which a party would expect to have.

Knowing what they do changes the way you read contracts to work out things such as:

- The legal effect of the contract and how it's likely to be interpreted,

- whether you have the rights you thought you had or don't,

- whether there is a breach of contract,

- whether there are rights to terminate the contract and how they must be exercised,

- whether rights to damages are limited,

They establish legal relationships in contracts with more certainty, whether for or against you.

Boilerplate clauses often appear at the end of a contract, but they don't have to. They could be anywhere in the contract, disguised or embedded in a long tract of text, and be easy to miss.

Are Boilerplate Clauses Standard? Are they standard provisions of a contract?

Boilerplate clauses are often called "standard" and can be boring. You will only have to include them if you want the contract to do what you intend and have the legal effect you want it to have. The only way boilerplate clauses are standard is that it's a common practice to include clauses of that description, especially in business contracts. Like all contract clauses, boilerplate clauses are interpreted using **the precise words used in the clause**. Although some boilerplate clauses may look the same, they can have a significantly different legal effect. One word in the right place is all it takes to change the legal meaning completely, like using the word "not" or removing it where you'd ordinarily expect to see it. When it comes to interpretation of contracts, it may not be what the parties might have intended the boilerplate clause to mean.

It's what **a reasonable reader** of the contract would give it that counts. This is consistent with the well-entrenched principles of the interpretation of contracts:

- Each clause of a contract needs to be interpreted within the context of the whole contract

- Each boilerplate clause has its legal effect on its terms

- The effect it will have within the entire contract will depend on the other clauses of the contract, along with the background in the lead-up to signing the contract

Boilerplate clauses may have one or more purposes or effects, such as:

A. Extinguish or exclude claims under the contract where claims might ordinarily exist at law

a) Entire Agreement clause

Entire agreement clauses prevent parties in a contract from claiming that any earlier agreements or statements made during earlier discussions or negotiations form part of the final agreement. They ensure that the only terms that apply between the parties are those set out in the contract itself. As a result, entire agreement clauses create certainty between the parties regarding their contractual duties and obligations to each other. Without an entire agreement clause. there could be a side agreement that the parties are bound to comply with despite not being written into the contract. Entire agreement clauses are sometimes the subject of disputes whereby the party seeking to rely on them claims that the other cannot rely on pre-contractual representations. This makes them crucial in protecting parties by limiting their obligations to the terms identified in the contract itself.

b) Third Party Rights clause

In most countries, the law may provide rights that enable a third party to potentially enforce a contract in its favor and therefore express terms to exclude the effects of such laws are essential. A typical third-party rights clause limits the ability of a non-party to enforce the contract terms or prevents the third-party from receiving any benefits under the contract. A third-party rights clause can also remove the need for a non-party's agreement to a variation of the contract. Sometimes referred to as a "hold harmless" clause, this clause aims to specify which party is responsible for litigation brought by a third party. This is often meant as insurance for parties that hire contractors or other parties, they might regularly do business with.

B. Grant rights to a contracting party which are unknown or not recognized by the general law

a) Escrow Clause

Occasionally, compensation for a specific job is best held in a special account while the work is being completed. The escrow clause may also specify in which circumstances the escrow account may be touched, and by whom.

b) Termination clause:

At the time of signing the Contract agreement, both Bob and the contractor would be in a very happy and positive state of mind. Hence this condition is usually not given its due importance. However, at a later date, if there is a requirement to terminate this contract agreement, it becomes a challenge to agree on the method of doing so. For example, what would be the conditions under which either Bob or the contractor could terminate the contract? If either Bob or the Contractor has not performed their duties under the Contract, there is an obvious case for the aggrieved party to terminate the Contract agreement. If in case Bob does not have funds to complete the work, can the Contractor terminate the contract agreement? If there is a scenario like the Covid pandemic, can either Bob or the Contractor terminate the Contract agreement? If decisions are delayed by Bob on some aspect of the construction beyond a reasonable timeline, can the contractor terminate the contract? In case decisions are delayed, can the Contractor temporarily suspend the work? In such cases of either suspension or termination, how much time should be given by Bob to the Contractor or vice versa? Once the contract agreement is terminated, will the Contractor get any payments from Bob? Or if Bob realizes that he has overpaid the Contractor, how can he recover such excess payments made to the Contractor? It is in everyone's best interest to discuss and clarify all these points right at the beginning of the Contract agreement where all parties are in a positive and happy state of mind.

c) Suspension clause:

Can either Bob or the contractor suspend the works for any reasonable period? For example, if Bob faces some challenges in arranging funds for the project, can he suspend construction of the project? If the contractor does not receive payment from Bob on time, can he/she suspend the work? What happens during the period of suspension? Will the contractor be entitled to take away his machinery and materials from the construction location or will he/she have to leave it there itself? Can Bob use part of the constructed house during the period of suspension? How long can the suspension be effective? For example, if Bob suspends the construction for a period of 6 months, would it be fair for the contractor to work on the same terms and conditions as agreed earlier? If the contractor suspends the work for a period of 6 months, can Bob take certain actions and get the work executed by some other contractor? These are the aspects that need to be clarified within the contract agreement. What happens if the suspension of work is due to factors beyond the control of both Bob and the contractor? For example, the whole world has recently witnessed the COVID-19 pandemic and it has resulted in the suspension of all activities worldwide for quite a long time. In a similar situation, the works have been suspended due to no fault of either Bob or the contractor. However, both the parties suffer losses or delays. How would such situations be addressed in the contract? The standard terms and conditions cover these aspects in great detail and it is important to give a detailed thought on these aspects while entering into the contract agreement. Ensure that the contract agreement provides solution in every foreseeable situation to prevent any dispute which could result in losses and a strained relationship.

d) Force Majeure Clause:

While all of us would have heard about this term after the Covid pandemic, it is recommended that we go a bit deeper into this and understand the implications. It is important to define what constitutes Force majeure. Usually, force majeure is associated with conditions which are considered as Acts of "God". However, it could specifically include epidemic, lock downs, wars, riots, natural calamities, etc.

It is important to agree these events upfront. Further, just because a force majeure event has occurred, it need not result in termination of a contract. Both parties have duties to notify the other party about events and actions. It is their duties to take efforts to mitigate the effect of such force majeure event and then after a reasonable period evaluate the option of terminating the contract agreement. No matter whatever are the conditions, it is best to agree them upfront to prevent any possible disagreements or disputes at a later date.

A force majeure clause states that if an extreme, unforeseeable event occurs that prevents or delays a party from performing their contractual obligations that party will not be in breach of contract by any means. Typical examples of force majeure events include floods, earthquakes, epidemics etc.

If a party claims force majeure, the other party's corresponding obligations under the contract will also be suspended. For instance, if you are the supplier and the customer has claimed force majeure, you may no longer have to supply. Often a force majeure clause also sets out a timeframe after which, if the force majeure event is continuing, either party is able to serve notice to terminate so that the parties can make alternative commercial arrangements.

Force majeure clauses cannot be implied into a contract. If you want to rely on a force majeure clause, you must check the contract to see if the clause exists. In the current economic climate, it is likely that we may also see an increase in parties seeking to rely on force majeure and therefore it is important that you ensure your contract includes the necessary wording.

C. Enable or disable entitlements which would otherwise be granted by law, by default

a) Assignment clause

This clause will specifically indicate that the terms under the contract cannot be assigned to another party. It may first indicate that the parties warrant to one another that they haven't assigned any rights or duties under the contract to a third party. It will then go on to indicate that the clause restricts the ability of either party to subcontract their duties under the contract. For example, a lease contract might provide that the lessee cannot sublet his or her construction equipment to a third party, even if that third party agrees to submit a monthly lease payment to the owner of the construction equipment. In case of a construction contract, it is possible that the contract agreement provides for the Buyer to assign the contract. This means that if Bob decides to assign his contract to someone else, the Contractor would now have a new Buyer instead of Bob after the assignment is completed. Now would the Contractor be comfortable with this right being available to Bob or vice versa? This is best clarified in the Contract.

b) Subcontracting clause

This clause is intended to clarify the following:

i) Can the Contractor sub contract the entire section of his works to some other organization? This is for the Buyer to review. It is to protect the interests of the Buyer so that the Contractor who has been selected after a lot of due diligence does not sub contract the whole of the works to some other sub-contractor who may not be qualified to do the work.

ii) However, the contractor may need to sub contract part of the works or some specialized works. This clause can then allow certain works to be sub contracted by the Contractor and the same would be captured in the contract agreement

iii) Further during the execution of the works, there may be a need for the Contractor to sub contract certain additional works which was not foreseen prior to signing the contract agreement. This clause can also allow such additional sub-contracting after the explicit approval of the Buyer.

D. Confirm, restate, or modify the application of general rules of law to the contract

a) Severance clause:

If any part of the agreement is considered invalid in future, such clause prevents the entire agreement to be considered invalid. This is one of the most important boilerplate clauses in a commercial contract. The purpose of the severability clause is to indicate that if any provisions are deemed void or invalid, the entire contract is not deemed to be unenforceable. Rather, only that term or provision will be removed from the overall contract.

b) Time of the Essence clause:

This clause can be mentioned in case of specific projects that have to be completed within a specific date.

For example, if a Buyer wants to construct a hotel which he intends to open for business by Christmas season, there would be a specific requirement for the works to be completed prior to the festive season.

If the Contractor is unable to complete the project before the agreed date, the Buyer would incur losses and the intent of the project is not met. Hence this is an important clause when time is a critical factor.

c) Variation clause

The Agreement may only be amended or supplemented by a written format between the Parties. This clause will indicate that the contract can only be amended upon entering into another written contract that is signed by both parties. While this clause isn't required in a contract, it could be beneficial, particularly for a construction project wherein the project and scope of the work may be subject to change over the duration of the project. Therefore, if additional materials are required, more time is needed, or additional costs arise over the course of the construction project, both parties will be aware of the fact that any new terms and provisions must be in writing and signed by both parties. A variation clause sets out a procedure whereby the contract can be amended at a later date. The reason for their inclusion is to prevent informal or inadvertent changes to the contract and to help keep a track of changes, especially in long term contracts. Most long-term contracts may need variations as circumstances of the parties or the terms may change throughout the term.

Variation clauses usually set out how the variation can be done. Usually, this will be in writing and signed by both parties. Without the inclusion of a variation clause, the contract could be amended informally through speech or conduct, without writing or including a signature, potentially resulting in uncertainty and disagreement between the parties at a later stage.

Unless there is an agreement specifically permitting the contractor to bring variations in jobs requirements, it is usually Bob as the buyer who has the right to vary or change any of his requirements. It is important for the contract agreement to specify the way in which such changes to the buyer's requirements are addressed. For example, would Bob be able to change his requirements to a great extent? Initially, Bob wished to have his house constructed in 2 levels. However, going forward, he decided to add an additional floor. What would be the impact of this on both Bob and the Contractor? Would the contractor be able to construct the additional floor with the existing set of machineries or would the contractor have to bring some additional machinery? In such a case would the contractor be entitled to receive additional payments from Bob? How would such changes be communicated by Bob to the contractor? Does the contractor have a right to accept or deny such request for change? Can Bob instruct any other contractor to do works which have initially been agreed to be executed by the first contractor – perhaps due to possible commercial benefits for Bob? Does the first contractor have any rights under the contract to prevent Bob from taking such actions? It is in the best interest of Bob and the Contractor to check the respective contract agreement conditions which clarifies the above queries on the right to vary.

d) Survival clauses

Survival clauses are required because they focus on preserving the intention of the contract and the interests of the parties once the contract is over. They are often related to maintaining confidentiality, preventing misuse of the residual knowledge, non-disclosure of otherwise private details of the parties, etc.

The survival clauses are essentially present to ensure that the parties remain bound to the provisions of preservation and are maintaining security of information and knowledge.

e) Prevalence clause

This clause mentions the overriding effect of this agreement in comparison with any other agreement or document made in writing by the parties. It means that the clauses of this agreement shall prevail if any other document or agreement is in conflict with this agreement.

f) Dispute Resolution clause

Similar to the conditions relating to termination of the contract agreement, it is best to agree on the process, conditions, and timelines relating to the dispute resolution process at the initial stage of the contract agreement when the Parties are in a happy and positive state of mind. It would be in the best interest of both parties to pre-agree a process of settlement of any dispute. In some cases, it may be in the best interest to identify and agree to a mutually agreed third-party individual or organization to intervene in the event of a dispute. No matter what the conditions are, it is best to agree with them upfront to prevent any possible disagreements or disputes at a later date, as during a dispute, it may become difficult to agree with anything! As arbitration is the most commonly used alternative for dispute resolution, there is a good chance your business contract will address this possibility. Arbitration refers to settling a legal matter outside of court with a third party — the arbitrator — and letting them determine a resolution. The provision could state that any dispute will be settled by arbitration, or it could determine whether or not the decision or an outside arbitrator would be binding.

E. Avoid the application of undesirable laws

a) Choice of law clause

In the case of a contract breach, the parties need to decide which country's legal rules applies to them. This is especially important if each party is located in a different country. Since laws vary depending on the region, a party may want to choose a relevant clause that benefits them. Having said that, the countries in question need to have a connection with the parties or their business. There must be common grounds and relevance.

Governing Law and Jurisdiction clause provides that the agreement shall be governed by, and construed in accordance with, the laws of .... (Say India) and courts/ tribunals in .... (Say Delhi, India) shall have exclusive jurisdiction to settle any disputes which may arise out of or in connection with this agreement and the parties can irrevocably submit themselves to the exclusive jurisdiction of such courts/ tribunals.

Generally, if the parties in the agreement are persons residing in India and the agreement does not pertain to a cross-border transaction, the agreement should be governed by laws of India and the Indian courts shall have exclusive jurisdiction over the transaction by default. However, in the event the transaction has a cross-border effect or if one of the parties to the agreement is not an Indian resident, then the parties are at liberty to choose the governing law and the jurisdiction in which either of the parties resides or of a neutral third country law which is commercially viable.

b) Jurisdiction clause

Along with the choice of law, this clause defines in which state a suit must be filed in the case of a contract breach. If choosing a region where neither party operates, then there needs to be a relevant connection and reason. If both parties are in the state of Maharashtra (India) and selling coconuts from Kerala (India), their contract must still define that the case falls under Indian jurisdiction.

F. Preserve rights that would otherwise be lost

a) Waiver clause:

A waiver clause means that if a party has not used its right to enforce the terms of the contract, either by failing to enforce an obligation or following a breach of contract by the other party, the innocent party does not lose its right to enforce the terms at a later date.

A valid waiver by a Party shall be in writing and executed by an authorized representative of that Party.

Neither the failure by any Party to insist on the performance of the terms, conditions, and provisions of this Agreement nor time or other indulgence granted by any Party to the other Parties shall act as a waiver of such breach or acceptance of any variation or the relinquishment of any such right or any other right under this Agreement, which shall remain in full force and effect.

b) Set-Off clause

A set-off clause is a short clause sometimes included in a commercial contract, often found within the payments clause.

Example: "You agree that we may set-off or deduct from any monies payable to you under this Agreement, any amounts which are payable by you to us (whether under this Agreement or otherwise)."

At law, the rights granted under this kind of clause can be quite narrow. However, set-off clauses have the potential to give the Buyer a lot of extra rights they would not otherwise have.

What is the Impact of a Set-Off Clause?

A set-off clause allows a Buyer to deduct money from payments it owes to the service provider/Contractor. This deduction is permitted under certain circumstances, such as where:

i. the Contractor owes a debt to the Buyer; or

ii. the Buyer has suffered some loss and needs to be compensated.

For example, suppose that the Contractor, were to breach a third party's IP rights, resulting in a loss to the Buyer. The set-off clause allows the Buyer to subtract the amount owed by the Contractor from their payments. As a result of the subtraction, the Buyer will pay the net amount. This will be the full price listed in the contract, minus the damages resulting from the IP breach.

The above example may be a fair and reasonable deduction. However, other examples can cause inconvenience for Contractors.

Imagine you were working on a new project for a Buyer, and you have purchased materials, conducted the agreed work, and submitted your first invoice. In response, your invoice comes back with only half the amount paid. When you post a query about it, it appears that a broad set-off clause has allowed the Buyer to deduct money since they claim that some of your initial work was defective, and the cost to rectify the defect was 50% of your invoice price.

As a Contractor, the best way to manage a set-off clause in your contract is to ensure you read it carefully before signing off.

The goal of reading through or amending the set-off clause in your contract is to ensure that the right to set-off monies is as limited as possible. As a service provider, one of your main goals is to ensure you are paid on time and in full. A set-off clause, when drafted broadly, may inhibit this right.

However, amending a set-off clause at the contractual level does not eliminate a set-off right. Buyers may still maintain this right.

It is important to note that the equitable set-off right is not available in every dispute, as the right must be determined and settled by a court. In the scenario where a set-off right is contractually written in a contract, it is more difficult to avoid.

With that in mind, amending a set-off clause at the time of contracting is the best pathway forward. It is quite reasonable to request a Buyer to limit or eliminate the right of their set-off. A limited set-off right ensures a fair arrangement with your Buyers whilst still protecting your interests as a Contractor.

A set-off clause allows your Buyer to set-off or deduct any amounts you may owe them against the amounts they owe you. It can be a hidden right that catches you off guard and affects your cashflows as a Contractor.

c) Confidentiality

A confidentiality clause is imperative if the transaction between the parties involves the exchange or disclosure of either party's confidential information. Without this clause, only limited protection is given under law and this may not be sufficient for the parties.

A confidentiality clause is classed as 'confidential information', for example trade secrets, financial information or customer or supplier details. It can also set out how it can be used, what specific action is required to protect it, and agreeing a process for its return, destruction, or unavoidable disclosures.

This particular provision states that certain business operations performed under the contract are not to be discussed with outside parties. A common name for this is a non-disclosure agreement or NDA, which is common in other types of contracts besides business.

d) Notice clause

The notice clause specifies the manner in which notices are disseminated and delivered to the two parties. The notice clause touches on many other clauses because to amend the contract, you must properly notify the other party.

e) Parties Clause: In this clause, the details of both the parties are mentioned. For instance, in case of an individual- name of the party, father's name, age, address, PAN number, etc. are mentioned. In case of legal entity, name of the legal entity, name of laws under which it is incorporated, registered office, etc. are mentioned. Also, a particular term is devoted to each party which is used in the entire agreement for referring to such a party.

f) Background clause: This clause provides the commercial intention/ purpose of the parties to enter into an agreement

g) Definition and interpretation clause: Certain terms which are technical in nature or such words whose explanation is important to avoid confusion are defined under this clause to give clarity in interpretation of it.

h) Communications: this condition clearly specifies the protocol that should be followed for communications. For example, what would be the language of communication? Would it be English or any other local language that both parties would have agreed? What would be the accepted mode of communication? A few years back, it was recommended to have all formal communications to be transmitted through print media in physical form. However, we live in a digital age and email is largely accepted as a form of communication. In this particular contract, would the parties agree to communicate on email? Going forward there are other forms of communication such as a WhatsApp, Facebook, LinkedIn, etc. Would these forms of communication be considered as appropriate and acceptable from this particular contract? This needs to be clarified. For further communications happening over email, does it have to be from the official email ID of both organizations or would emails from a personal email ID be acceptable? Now, what if any of the things has to be delivered in physical form? Which address must be kept as the delivery address of both the parties? This needs to be clarified. Further, are there any time restrictions for such communications to be delivered at this particular address? For example, if it's an organization there could be certain working hours or certain hours in a day when such communications are being received. Beyond these hours, there is a possibility of not being able to receive parcels due to certain logistics issues. These need to be clarified in the contract agreement.

i) Statutory compliances: it is important to clarify who takes care of certain compliances. For example, usually in construction projects, the client or the buyer, in this case, Bob, would be responsible for arranging their own necessary compliances pertaining to the land on which the house is being constructed. However, it is possible that this responsibility could lie with the contractor. This needs to be clarified. The compliances are put to the land, and there could be approvals required from local authorities. It is important to clarify which party is responsible for this. In certain countries, a specific approval from the local authorities has to be acquired prior to the commencement of use of any property. For example, in certain locations, a certificate called an occupancy certificate is provided by the local authority. It is to be clarified who would need to obtain the local authority's approval.

j) Payment Schedule and currency of payment: While the compensation / amount is usually specified in every contract agreement as it is a basic element, there are other aspects relating to payments that must also be specified to avoid any disagreements or disputes at a later date. For example, let us assume that Bob has agreed to pay the Contractor an amount of $100,000 for constructing his dream house over a period of, say, 12 months. Would the Contractor have to wait for the entire 12 months for Bob to pay him the full amount, or would Bob be required to pay some parts of the amount at some pre-agreed frequency? Would the Contractor require any advance amounts for preparatory works before actually starting works at the construction site? What happens if the Contractor does not commence the works after Bob has paid him some advances? Or what happens if the Contractor utilizes the amounts provided by Bob as an advance for some other purpose? Would the Contractor be able to do so? What preventive measures can Bob take to prevent such steps from being taken by the Contractor? Are there any laws that prevent such cases from occurring? These aspects would need to be specifically considered in every contract agreement. Further, depending on the complexity of the contract, it may be a possibility that the payments may be made in multiple currencies. For example, if Bob wants his Contractor to import some expensive item from another country, the payment will be made based on currency conversion rates. It may be in the Contractor's best interest to specify such amounts in the currency with which the Contractor intends to buy such items to mitigate any currency fluctuation risks. It may also be in Bob's interest to ensure that these amounts are agreed in a different currency to ensure that he pays for the exact amount with some reasonable service charges for the Contractor's services. It would be important for the Contract agreement to specify these conditions upfront while signing the Contract.

k) Insurances: There are multiple types of insurance that may be required in a project. For example, some insurances cover the machinery, materials, and workmen who are associated with the specific construction works. However, what happens to materials that are in transit? Let us consider that the Contractor has imported certain materials from an outside country, and the same is being transported through a cargo ship. If there is any mishap that happens to this ship and the said materials are lost or damaged, how would the Contractor or Bob be affected? Who would need to insure such materials? Similarly, what happens to workers who are contributing remotely to the construction? For example, if there is some product which is manufactured by a contractor at his factory and some workmen are working in his factory, who is responsible for insuring such workmen? These aspects need to be clarified in the Contract agreement

Summary

There are many other boilerplate clauses that can be included; however, not every contract needs every possible one. It is important while preparing a contract to understand which are the most relevant ones and their purpose and effect. Although we have explained some of the most common boilerplate clauses used in commercial contracts, it's always sensible to get sound advice from an experienced commercial solicitor to understand which are most relevant and important for your contract. Also, while considering any boilerplate clause, the need would be to see if it is required. You will also have to analyze the effect of its language and figure out the applicable law before incorporating the same into the agreement.

Importance of Boilerplate clauses

1. Boilerplate clauses are often considered to be of less importance. However, its significance is recognized when there is some hindrance in the smooth functioning of obligations by the parties.

2. Boilerplate clauses are important when there are any differences or disputes between parties.

3. Boilerplate clauses give parties a method to move forward and complete their obligations as mentioned in the agreement in compliance to all the rules and regulations when there are disputes or differences between the parties.

4. A well-drafted boilerplate clause results in smooth functioning and execution of the contract between the parties.

5. Since well-drafted boilerplate clauses help smooth execution, it saves lots of time and litigation costs.

Consequence of Overlooking Boilerplate Clauses

1. In case of differences/disputes, parties often regret inserting a practical and favorable boilerplate clause.

2. Neglecting the boilerplate clauses can lead to unintended legal consequences.

3. It causes a lack of clarity during disputes or differences between parties.

4. Finding relevance in the standard boilerplate clauses often wastes a lot of time.

5. Standard boilerplate clauses copied from other generic agreements often fail to solve the dispute/difference between the parties.

Conclusion

Generally, parties are ignorant to take a glance at boilerplate clauses and modify it according to their satisfaction. The lawyer who is assisting the parties in drafting and executing the final contract must emphasize the importance and legal consequences.

There exists a number of boilerplate clauses, but one needs to understand which among these clauses are necessary for their agreement, keeping in mind the facts and subject matter of the agreement.

Boilerplate clauses have an important place in a contract and one cannot afford to overlook them. These boilerplate clauses often gain its importance when parties are in a dispute.

Therefore, it is recommended that one should not just 'cut and paste' them from other standard agreements.

You can undoubtedly say that boilerplate clauses are as important as operative clauses of contract such as representations and warranties of parties, consideration, term, scope, condition precedent, condition subsequent, etc.

While we have discussed the important clauses that are required to be added to any contract agreement, sometimes it becomes embarrassing for both parties to discuss certain difficult conditions like dispute resolution and termination aspects at the time of signing the contract agreement. In some cases, both parties choose to remain silent during difficult conditions just to avoid embarrassing discussions. Well, if the parties choose to remain silent, someone else may decide their fate.

Call To Action:

You are now requested to refer your agreements and see if the above-mentioned boiler plate clauses are covered with the same or if there are any new boiler plate clauses that have been incorporated.

For a list of typical boiler plate clauses, you may visit www.prasamviidah.com

CHAPTER 3:

STANDARD FORMS OF CONTRACTS

Overview

We have covered the process of selecting a contractor and getting into an agreement. We have also seen the crucial conditions or clauses that must be discussed and captured within the Contract agreement. Apart from the essential requirements addressed in the previous chapters, multiple clauses may seem insignificant but can assume significance in a dispute. So, if Bob or the contractor are not signing contract agreements daily, how do they ensure that all the required conditions are discussed and captured appropriately within the contract agreement? Do they have to write each Contract from scratch, or is there any easier way to draft it? Who would draft the Contract – will it be Bob as a "Buyer" or the "Contractor" who needs to draft a contract agreement?

Thankfully, when it comes to construction contracts, there are quite a few standard forms of contract documents that reputed international organizations publish, and we can now discuss these in detail in the later part of this chapter.

Before we get into the standard contract documents that reputed international organizations publish, we can look at the legal overview of using the Standard Forms of Contracts. In this technological age where a company makes contracts in thousands of numbers daily, it takes work to make them from scratch. Generally, a consumer or a person who signs a contract rarely reads the terms and conditions written in the Contract. Even if they read it, it may be challenging to understand most of the agreement's terms and conditions, making it difficult to protect the weaker party. Standard forms of Contract are done on national and international levels, and the same challenges exist everywhere.

The standard form of Contract is generally perceived as a 'take it or leave it.' In this type of Contract, one party is not in a position to negotiate the terms and conditions laid down in the agreement, and this party usually has the option of either entering into the Contract or not entering into the Contract. Thus, this type of arrangement may affect the fundamental right to negotiate. The most common types of standard forms of contracts are insurance company contracts, purchasing a washing machine, signing up for your email, social networking sites, etc.

The Indian contract system does not have any specific differentiation between standard forms of Contract and general Contract, as the common form of Contract is a kind of Contract that is governed by the laws provided for public contracts in the Indian Contract Act 1872. However, in many countries, the judiciary is empowered to apply the principle of natural justice and give good justice to the weaker party. It may appear easy to exploit the party entering into the standard form of Contract. Hence, specific rules are made to protect the interests of the weaker party. For example:

1. A reasonable notice must be given by the person delivering the document to provide adequate information about the terms and conditions laid down in the Contract.

2. Notice of the terms and conditions should be given before or at the time of Contract when it is to be signed.

3. Misrepresentation, fraud, mischief, and other elements that make a contract void should not be present in the Contract to make an agreement enforceable by law.

4. Pointing out unreasonable terms in the Contract can be a protective safeguard for the weaker party. Unreasonable terms of the Contract can be said about those terms in the Contract that contradict the purpose of the Contract or are against public policy.

5. In some instances, in the case of breach of Contract, the weaker party will not be bound to follow the Contract in case of contract violation by the other party.

6. The Contract is between the two parties who have contracted with each other, and no third party is entitled to enjoy the right provided in the Contract nor hold any liability. As the third party is not responsible for the irregularity in the Contract, he is not entitled to any benefit from the Contract.

Now, why use standard forms of Contracts?

Before we get to the standard forms of Contracts that are available for us to use, let us examine the advantages and disadvantages of using the standard forms of contracts. There are several advantages to using a standard contract form. Some of these advantages are as follows:

1. Familiarity with the standard forms of Contract: As various stakeholders use the standard forms of Contract multiple times and they mostly contain the same terms, it becomes familiar for all the stakeholders, making it easier for even a non-technical/nonlegal person to understand and trust the meanings of the conditions mentioned therein.

2. Reduced transaction costs: By using a standard form of Contract, there is no need to make customized or bespoke contracts, thereby reducing transaction costs for all parties involved.

3. Expedites the process: With the use of standard forms of contracts, there is no need to get into the tedious process of drafting contracts from scratch, carrying out detailed negotiations, etc. Familiarity with the standard forms of contracts by all stakeholders involved reduces the time taken in negotiation, and the entire contract agreement can be concluded very quickly.

The goal is to use standard contracts for anyone conducting similar business transactions. Standard forms are popular because they are used to facilitate common business transactions efficiently and cost-effectively. These contracts are usually many pages long, with details outlining the terms and conditions. Standard contracts are frequently used when vendors and consumers routinely participate in legally and technically complex transactions. While there are many benefits to standard forms, there are issues and risks with them as well.

Challenges associated with standard form of contracts relate to:

1. Consent

In the case of commercial contracts, courts have repeatedly held that contracts, even if entered into the standard format, are meant to be performed and not to be avoided. Unless it is shown that consent is obtained by fraud, mistake, or duress, consent given by a party to a contract is legally valid. As defined under Section 13 of the Contract Act of 1872, two or more persons are said to consent when they agree upon the same thing in the same sense. According to Section 14, consent is free when it is not caused by coercion, undue influence, fraud, misrepresentation, or mistake. Thus, courts have refused to interfere where the parties with equal bargaining powers have fairly consented to the terms of the Contract without any fraud, duress, or mistake.

2. Unfair terms of the contract

Courts have looked into the terms of the Contract in relation to the parties' bargaining powers and have interfered in cases where the parties' bargaining power was not equal. If a contract or a clause in a contract is found unreasonable, unfair, or irrational, one must look to the relative negotiating power of the contracting parties. This principle is that the courts may not enforce and, when called upon to do so, strike down an unfair and unreasonable contract or an unfair and unreasonable clause in a contract between parties who are not equal in negotiating power. It is difficult to give an exhaustive list of all negotiations of this type. No organization can visualize the different situations which can arise in the commercial affairs. One can only attempt to give some examples. For example, the above principle will apply where the inequality of negotiating power results from the great disparity in the economic strength of the contracting parties. It will apply where the inequality results from circumstances, whether of the creation of the parties or not. It will apply to situations in which the weaker party is in a position where he can obtain goods, services, or means of livelihood only upon the terms imposed by the stronger party or go without them. It will also apply where an organization has no choice, or rather no meaningful choice, but to give their consent to a contract to, sign on the dotted line in a prescribed or standard from, or to accept a set of rules as part of the Contract, however unfair, unreasonable a clause in that Contract or form or regulations may be.

This principle, however, will not apply where the negotiating power of the contracting parties is equal or almost equal. This principle may not apply where both parties are businessmen and the Contract is a commercial transaction. In today's complex world of giant corporations with their vast infra-structural organizations and with the government through its instrumentalities and agencies entering into almost every branch of industry and commerce, multiple situations can result in unfair and unreasonable bargains between parties possessing wholly disproportionate and unequal negotiating power. These cases must be enumerated and fully illustrated. However, the principle can be followed while drafting contracts.

Thus, courts may enforce and strike down an unfair and unreasonable contract or clause in a contract between parties who are not equal in negotiating power. This principle, however, will not apply where the bargaining power of the contracting parties is equal or almost equal or where both parties are businessmen and the Contract is a commercial transaction. In further cases where the terms of the Contract are unreasonable as to the nature of the Contract, courts have struck them out following the principles laid down under the Contract Act or common law.

There is a minimum duty of care imposed upon all service providers under Section 151 of the Contract Act, and they cannot contract themselves out of and is not subject to any contract to the contrary between the parties. Once that minimum duty is imposed upon the laundry by the law, a breach of that duty undoubtedly protects the party affected with the right to recover damages commensurate with the consequences".

3. One sided nature of the contract

The basic test of "one sidedness" of the Contract is whether, under the circumstances existing at the time of the making of a contract, in light of the general commercial background and commercial needs of a particular trade or case, the clauses involved are so one-sided as to oppress or unfairly suppress the other party.

4. Inequality of negotiating powers

Where the parties are put on unequal terms, the standard form of Contract cannot be said to be the subject matter of negotiation between the parties, and the same is said to have been dictated by the party whose higher bargaining power enables him to do so.

5. Battle of the forms and standard form contracts

Using standard-form contracts can lead to a battle over whose form is to be used. Consider the following situation: The manager of an organization (Buyer) emails a Supplier (Seller) requesting a quote for supplying paper bags with the Buyer's standard form contract attached. The seller replies by providing a quotation with its standard form contract attached. Usually, everything will run smoothly, and the question of whose legal form the contract applies will not become an issue. However, when something goes wrong (Defective product—failure to pay or anything) the battle of the forms makes the issue all the more difficult, time-consuming, and expensive to resolve. Therefore, it is essential to ensure that when different standard forms are being passed around, the parties agree on whose standard form is to be the Contract for the transaction.

One of the disadvantages observed is the use of legal jargon, as some of these standard forms of contracts use legal terminologies. A non-technical/non-legal person may need help to understand the meaning or interpretation of every single word completely. The understanding of a word we have in English may have a different meaning in a legal context. So, even if one reads word by word, it may be a challenge for a common man to comprehend the entire text. This leaves a layman with two options: either to hire a legal expert and have the Contract interpreted to them, which is going to cost money, time, and effort, or to go into the Contract with incomplete understanding, which might leave them at a disadvantage at a later stage.

Furthermore, these contracts are so detailed and long, consumers often sign the agreement without reading the fine prints. Usually, the terms in standard form contracts often benefit the party with the most negotiating power. This type of uneven purchasing power exists between businesses and consumers. When there are inequalities in the ability to negotiate, it results in an agreement that works economically against one of the parties. In these cases, the courts advocate for the weaker party. If the Contract does not genuinely lookout for the best interests of all parties, the courts may intervene.

In order to overcome this disadvantage, there is an arrangement where the Parties to any contract agreement can mutually agree to amend certain conditions to suit their particular requirement. These are called special conditions of Contract or specific conditions of Contract and are usually mirrored on the basis of the Standard forms of Contract. Though it is easy to amend each and every condition of the standard form of contract, care and perhaps expert legal advice has to be taken prior to amending such standard conditions. Hence, by and large, it is convenient for all stakeholders involved to use a standard form of Contract with amendments to certain conditions based on the specific agreement requirements.

Construction contracts are of a complex nature and are included among the few types of contracts which have to be in writing. A construction contract is an agreement with a person or an organization to carry out or arrange for carrying out a construction operation, or providing for his own labor. Agreements to do architectural, design, or surveying works and agreements to provide consultancy in construction-related fields are also included under construction contracts.

Traditionally, contracts are negotiated between the parties to carry out each project separately. However, standard forms of contracts were introduced to make the industry more efficient. Some of the standard contract forms include FIDIC, Joint Contracts Tribunal (J.C.T. contracts), and Institute of Civil Engineers (I.C.E. contracts). If you are undertaking building work, you should ensure that you have a construction contract in place. There are several different types of standard-form arrangements, and you must ensure that the agreements' terms are fair and reasonable.

A well-drafted construction contract is helpful to provide certainty for both parties concerning a construction project. Construction works involve a unique risk profile, which makes them different from other commercial arrangements. A construction contract will allocate these construction-specific risks and liabilities between the parties.

Standard form contracts are industry standards and are often used because most participants in the construction industry will have some familiarity with them. Standard-form contracts can be used without requiring substantial change. However, they are often amended by parties, often extensively.

What are the standard forms available for us to use?

The global construction industry is familiar with a few standard forms of Contract, some listed and explained below. The below-mentioned standard forms of Contract are by no means an exhaustive list and is only an indicative list of some of the most popular forms of Contract used globally.

1. **FIDIC (Fédération Internationale Des Ingénieurs-Conseils),** which means the international federation of consulting engineers is a consulting organization based in Geneva, Switzerland. FIDIC publishes a variety of standards some of popular ones of which are listed below:

FIDIC publishes certain popular standard forms of construction contracts as:

a) **Green Book** – The Short Form of Contract
b) **Red Book** - Conditions of Contract for Construction for Building and Engineering Works designed by the Employer
c) **Yellow Book** - Contract Conditions for Plant & Design-Build for Electrical & Mech. Plant & For Building & Engineering Works Designed by the Contractor.

d) **Gold Book -** Conditions of Contract for Design, Build and Operate Project

e) **Silver Book -** Conditions of Contract for E.P.C. (Engineering, Procurement and Construction) Turnkey Projects

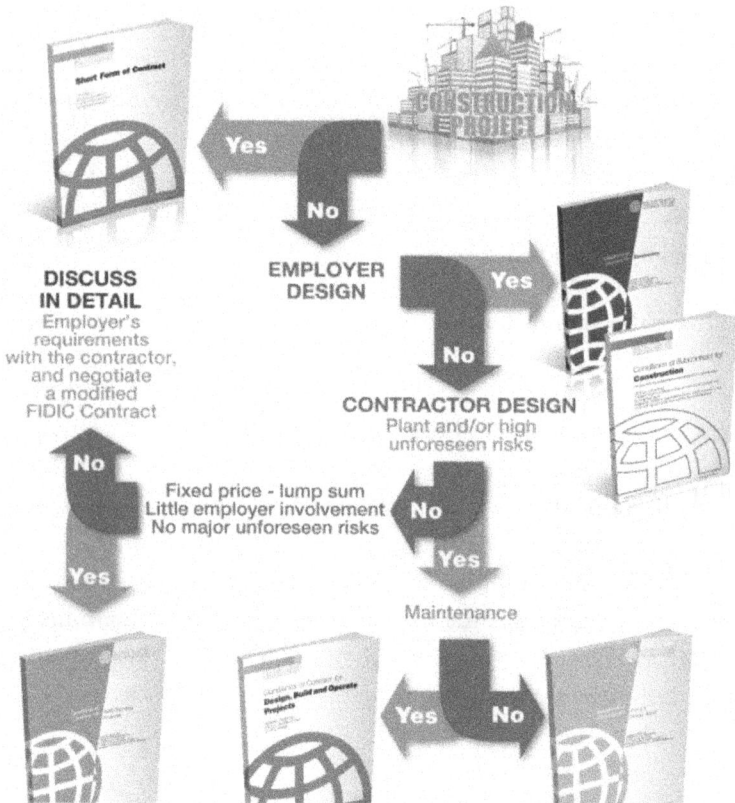

Source: www. fidic.org

FIDIC also publishes many guidance notes, training materials, etc., to help the stakeholders understand the various publications and make their own choices and amendments. They also amend the standard forms of Contracts from time to time based on feedback from industry practitioners. More details on the FIDIC forms of Contract can be obtained from www.fidic.org

NEC Contracts

The NEC Contract is another series of contracts designed to manage any project from start to finish. It is a system created by the United Kingdom Institute of Civil Engineers. Similar to the FIDIC publications, N.E.C. also has a wide range of standard forms of Contract as below:

Source: www.neccontract.com

The NEC4 Design Build and Operate Contract (DBOC) appoints a single contractor to design, build, operate, or maintain (but not fund) a client's asset over a defined service period. It can also be used when a client wants an existing asset operated by the contractor while it is being upgraded or extended.

The NEC4 Alliance Contract is a multi-party contract for appointing several partners to create an alliance to deliver a major project or program of work. Contracting as an alliance offers a different approach to collaborative working between Clients and suppliers compared with other types of Contracts. An alliance contract suits Clients who wish to enter into a longer-term collaborative contract with several suppliers in order to deliver a large scale multi discipline project or program of work.

The NEC4 Dispute Resolution Service Contract (DRSC) is for parties to NEC4 contracts to jointly appoint an adjudicator or members of a dispute avoidance board, to resolve a contractual dispute. It can also be used for setting a dispute resolver under other forms of Contract.

The NEC4 Engineering and Construction Contract (E.C.C.) is the main work contract in the NEC4 suite of collaborative, flexible, and clearly written contracts for built environment procurement. The E.C.C. can include any level of design. It has six main payment Options: A (priced Contract with activity schedule), B (priced

Contract with bill of quantities), C (target contract with activity schedule), D (target contract with bill of quantities), E (cost reimbursable contract) and F (management contract).

The NEC4 Engineering and Construction Short Contract (ECSC) is a simpler alternative to the NEC4 Engineering and Construction Contract (E.C.C.). The ECSC is for projects that are relatively easy to manage, comprise straightforward work, and impose only low risks on both the client and contractor.

The NEC4 Facilities Management Contract (F.M.C.) is intended to be used to appoint a service provider for some time to manage and provide a facility management service.

The NEC4 Framework Contract (F.C.) is intended to appoint one or more suppliers over a set term to carry out work or to provide a service or goods on an 'as instructed' basis using NEC4 contracts.

The NEC4 Professional Service Contract (P.S.C.) is the leading professional service contract in the NEC4 suite of collaborative, flexible, and clearly written contracts for built environment procurement. It is for appointing any provider of professional services, including project managers, service managers, supervisors, designers, and other consultants associated with an NEC4 contract. NEC4 PSC offers three main payment Options: A (priced Contract with activity schedule), C (target contract), and E (cost-reimbursable Contract). In Option A, most of the risk is placed with the service provider, while in Option C, it is shared between the client and service provider, and in Option E rests mostly with the client.

The NEC4 Supply Contract (S.C.) is for local and international purchases of high-value goods and related services, including design and training. Examples include significant items of plant, such as turbines, generators, transformers, pumps, rolling stock, cranes, gantries, and tunnel boring machines.

The above-mentioned standard forms of Contract are only an indicative list of publications by this organization. More details on the conditions of the Contract published by this organization can be obtained from www.neccontract.com.

2. International Chamber of Commerce (ICC)

Source: www.library.iccwbo.org

I.C.C. Model contracts and clauses aim to provide a sound legal basis upon which parties to international contracts can quickly establish an even-handed agreement acceptable to both sides. Like other organizations, I.C.C. also publishes standard forms of Contracts, some of the popular ones of which are listed below:

a) ICC Model Contract (International Sale – Manufactured goods)

The I.C.C. Model International Sale Contract is a time-saving tool for traders, business people, lawyers, and all parties involved in important import/export- and cross-border sales transactions.

It applies mainly to the sale of manufactured goods but can serve as an example to work on for other types of products as well.

b) The ICC Model Contract for the Turnkey Supply of an Industrial Plant

The Model Contract for the Turnkey Supply of an Industrial Plant has unique characteristics. The supplier's primary obligation is to supply the equipment and assist the purchaser during erection and startup. The supplier performs its obligations within facilities under the purchaser's control.

This I.C.C. Model Contract considers all of these specifics and contains enough flexibility for the parties to work out special situations for themselves. To leave the greatest possible space to alternative solutions, many issues (for example, raw materials, time schedule, erection equipment, etc.) are covered in the useful annexes.

In addition to the above there are other standard forms of contracts like:

c) ICC Model Commercial Agency Contract
d) ICC Model International Franchising Contract
e) ICC Model Mergers and Acquisitions Contract
f) ICC Model International Trademark License
g) ICC Model International Distributorship Contract
h) ICC Model Confidentiality Agreement
i) ICC Short form Model Contracts
j) ICC Model Online B2C General Conditions of Sale
k) ICC Model Contract Joint Venture

These above-mentioned standard forms of Contracts are periodically updated.

3. Joint Contracts Tribunal (JCT) Contracts

Source: www.jctltd.co.uk/

Since 1931 J.C.T. has produced standard forms of construction contract, guidance notes and other standard forms of documentation for use by the construction industry. Some of the popular standard forms published by J.C.T. are as below:

a) Standard Building Contract

The J.C.T. Standard Building Contract is designed for large or complex construction projects requiring detailed contract provisions. Standard Building Contracts are suitable for projects procured by traditional or conventional methods.

b) Intermediate Building Contract

The J.C.T. Intermediate Building Contract is designed for construction projects involving all the recognized trades and skills of the industry, where reasonably detailed contract provisions are needed, but without complex building service installations or other specialist work.

c) Minor Works Building Contract

The J.C.T. Minor Works Building Contract is designed for smaller, basic construction projects where the work is simple.

d) Design and Build Contract

The J.C.T. Design and Build Contract is designed for construction projects where the contractor carries out the design and the construction work. Design and build projects can vary in scale, but the Design and Build Contract is generally suitable where detailed provisions are needed.

e) Management Building Contract

The J.C.T. Management Building Contract is designed for construction projects where the employer appoints a management contractor to oversee the works. Construction is completed under separate works contracts, which the management contractor establishes and manages for a fee. Management building contracts are suitable for projects procured via the management method.

f) JCT – Construction excellence Contract (CE)

J.C.T. has collaborated with Constructing Excellence to develop the J.C.T. – Constructing Excellence Contract. The J.C.T. – Constructing Excellence Contract can be used to procure a range of construction services and is specifically tailored for use in partnering and where participants wish to have collaborative and integrated working practices.

g) Repair and maintenance contract

J.C.T.'s Repair and Maintenance Contract is designed for individual projects involving a defined program of repair and maintenance works to specified buildings or sites. This Contract is primarily for use by local authorities and other employers who regularly place small and medium-sized contracts for jobbing work and are sufficiently experienced that an independent contract administrator is optional.

The above-mentioned standard forms of contract are those that are used in multiple countries and have a global presence. Apart from those mentioned above, few countries have their standard conditions of Contract.

One such example is that of Sri Lanka. The Construction Industry Development Authority under the Ministry of Urban Development and Housing, Sri Lanka, has published various standard forms of contracts for construction projects in Sri Lanka. Details of the standard forms of Contracts published by this organization can be found in www.cida.gov.lk

In India, the Central Public Works Department publishes standard forms of Contract for use in their construction projects. The details of these are available in www.cpwd.gov.in Each of the above-referred examples of standard forms of contracts are from the construction industry.

However, other sectors also have legal agreements that can be referred to. Specific large organizations develop their own standard forms of contracts.

Standard forms of contract in global context and international usage

At this moment let us also look at the practices being followed in a few countries across the world. (Source: Reference number 23)

1. Angola

About public works, there are standard form contracts enacted by the Public Procurement Office **(Gabinete da Contratação Pública)**, but the use of such forms is not mandatory. In addition, some private construction and engineering sector associations provide auxiliary standard form contracts to their members. Usually, FIDIC forms are only used by major contractors and in international agreements.

International contract forms such as FIDIC and N.E.C. are commonly used, mainly in large-scale projects. Some locally structured agreements may also be available.

2. Australia

The Australian infrastructure market is dominated by standard-form contracts prepared and issued by various industry bodies. Both government and the private sector use these standard forms, have a widely understood risk allocation, and have often been the subject of judicial comment. The most commonly used legal forms are:

- Australian Standards contracts (issued by Standards Australia) – Australian Standards forms range from construct only to design and construct, construction management, supply, and subcontract

- Australian Building Industry Contract (ABIC) – a joint publication of the Master Builders Association and the Royal Australian Institute of Architects.

- Forms issued by the Master Builders Association (M.B.A.) – the M.B.A. has offices in each state and territory.

- Forms issued by the Housing Industry Association – usually used for smaller and residential projects.

- NPWC (National Public Works Committee) standard form construct-only Contract – used by several government agencies.

- GC-21 (N.S.W. Government) – suitable for construction contracts in a number of different circumstances: for projects valued at more than A$1M, at less than A$1M, for minor works around A$50,000, and for consultancy services

- Some forms of Contract more commonly used outside Australia are also occasionally used on Australian projects, such as:

- FIDIC conditions of Contract (E.P.C., design-build, Construction, electrical and mechanical, and civil engineering) – are occasionally used, particularly on large infrastructure projects involving offshore contractors.

- The N.E.C. suite

While most standard forms are periodically updated and reissued, many of the commonly used forms could be a few years old. As a result, they are typically amended by the insertion of special conditions to tailor or adjust the risk allocation, consider legislative change, or address project-specific needs. It is now unusual for any major project to be delivered using a standard form contract that has yet to be amended to suit the particular project. Many large employers have their own 'standard form' contract, which incorporates detailed special conditions to address project and risk requirements and specific commercial drivers. While some government agencies have now developed template contract forms and guidelines for the delivery of alliance projects, there are limited options for commercially available standard form contracts applicable to conditions of delivery such as alliance contracting, public-private partnerships (P.P.P.), or hybrid forms such as 'Early Contractor Involvement' (E.C.I.). These are generally prepared on a project-by-project basis. Some agencies that use these procurement methods frequently will tend to use the same form of Contract repetitively. Most government agencies that procure infrastructure have suites of standard contracts for use on their projects. Except FIDIC and N.E.C., other international forms of Contract are rarely used in Australia.

3. Belgium

Various industry bodies, private and public organizations, and/or associations supporting the Belgian Construction and engineering sector provide standard form contracts to their members. However, the use of such forms is not mandatory.

International conditions of Contract, such as some of the FIDIC contracts, are increasingly used in Belgium, although not currently commonly.

The selection of the form of an engineering and construction contract is generally dependent upon several factors, which include but are not limited to i) The timeframe of the project, ii) The expected costs and margin of unexpected costs, and iii) Whether or not the project is private or public.

4. Botswana

International contract forms such as FIDIC are used mainly in Public and Mining Sector projects and to a minimal extent in Private Sector projects.

A locally developed agreement (Botswana Institute of Development Professions form commonly referred to as the BIDP) is widely used in addition to the JBCC suite of contract forms developed in South Africa. These documents, and other alternatives, are available from professional organizations in the Botswana and S.A. construction industries.

5. Canada

Using standard form contracts on construction projects in Canada is quite common. One of the most widely used sources of standard forms is the Canadian Construction Documents Committee (CCDC). The CCDC publishes several different types of construction contracts that they have developed in consultation with representatives from all construction industry sectors. CCDC contract forms are endorsed by the Association of Consulting Engineering Companies (Canada), the Canadian Construction Association, Construction Specifications Canada, and the Royal Architectural Institute of Canada (RAIC).

In addition to the contracts published by the CCDC, specific professional organizations in Canada produce their industry-specific standard forms.

The RAIC, for example, publishes a standard form of contract between consultants and architects and a standard form between architect and client, among other standard forms. Certain provincial bodies produce their own standard forms, and various international standard forms may also be adopted in Canada.

6. China

The two most commonly used standard-form construction agreements are FIDIC's Conditions of Contract for Construction (the New Red Book) and China's Standard Form of Construction Contract.

The selection of the Contract often depends on the nationality of the parties. Generally, local contractors prefer to use China's Standard Form of Construction Contract as it is more concise. However, foreign developers are generally more familiar with FIDIC's Red Book.

7. Croatia

There is no national body or organization that produces standard form contracts for the construction and engineering sector. However, the General Practice (Usages) in Construction, which were adopted in 1977, are still applicable as a customary law source. The contract form also depends on whether it is concluded with a public body (where specific regulation on either public procurement or public-private partnerships applies) or between private persons, where often the FIDIC model agreement is used.

8. Czech Republic

The Czech Agency for Standardization (ČAS) has created standard Fidic-based work contracts and other documents.

- Czech contract standard (Design-Bid-Build)
- Czech contract standard (Design-Build)
- Special contract terms for construction
- BIM protocol

9. Denmark

In Denmark, standard-form building contracts go back more than 100 years. Four legal form building contracts are used in Denmark:

1. AB 18 – General Conditions for the provision of works and supplies within building and engineering.
2. A.B.T. 18 – General conditions for turnkey contracts.
3. A.B.R. 18 – General conditions for consulting services.

Note: A.B. Consumer – 'General conditions for the provisions of works within building to consumers. (A standard form contract that considers that the employer is a non-professional party.) These standard form building contracts are updated versions of the formerly used AB 92, A.B.T. 93, and A.B.R. 89 documents, drafted by the recommendations made by a committee set up by the Danish Ministry of Housing with a cross-section of representatives from the construction industry. However, international forms of Contract (such as FIDIC) are used in Denmark primarily within the off-shore/energy sector and large-scale infrastructure projects.

10. France

Various industry bodies, private and public organizations, and/or associations supporting the French Construction and engineering sector provide standard form contracts to their members. However, using such forms is not mandatory. International conditions of Contract, such as some of the FIDIC contracts, are increasingly, although not currently commonly used in France. The selection of the form of an engineering and construction contract is generally dependent upon several factors, which include but are not limited to: the timeframe of the project; the expected costs and extent of unexpected costs: whether or not the project is private or public in nature.

11. Germany

The Construction Contract Procedures (VOB) were developed by the German Procurement Committee for Construction Works (formerly the German Procurement Committee for Public Works Contracts).

Since the general law on contracts for work and services contained in the Civil Code is only of limited suitability in equally satisfying the interests of the contractor and the principal in construction law, the VOB was put in place.

It is regarded as a valuable instrument for properly reconciling the parties' interests to a construction contract (principal and contractor).

The VOB consists of three parts:

- **Part A:** 'General provisions on the procurement of contracts for construction work' – which contains the principal regulations on procurement law.
- **Part B:** 'General contractual conditions for the performance of construction work' contains several provisions differing from those of the Civil Code.
- However, the requirements of the Civil Code remain applicable up to the extent that they are not replaced by adequate provisions of the VOB/B. The goal of the VOB/B is to provide a balanced set of construction contract regulations that suit the interests of both contracting parties.
- **Part C:** 'General technical contractual conditions for construction work.'

Provisions released by FIDIC (the International Federation of Consulting Engineers) have limited relevance for construction contracts in Germany since the VOB/B is a useful instrument. Public authorities must use the VOB/B in construction contracts they enter into. However, in contracts for engineering, procurement, and construction services and for projects in foreign countries, FIDIC is widely used by German contractors.

12. Ghana

In addition to international contract forms such as FIDIC and NEC Contracts, the World Bank Conditions of Contract are recognized. Other agreements, such as the Ghana Public Procurement Board's Conditions of Contract for Procurement of Works and the General Conditions for Works Contracts financed by the European

Development Fund (E.D.F.), are commonly used. These documents and other alternatives are available partially online and from professional organizations in the Ghanaian construction industry.

13. Hong Kong, SAR

Institutional standard forms are issued by public and local authorities and sanctioned by the construction institutions.

Examples include:

- Agreement and Schedule of Conditions of Building Contract for Use in Hong Kong – Standard Form of Building Contract (Private Edition), issued under the sanction of the Hong Kong Institute of Architects / Hong Kong Institute of Surveyors ("HKIS");
- Joint Contracts Committee (JCC);
- Standard Form of Building Contract (JCT);
- Institute of Civil Engineers (ICE) Conditions of Contract Measurement Version;
- ICE Design and Construct Conditions of Contract;
- ICE New Engineering Contract (now known as NEC); and
- International Federation of Consulting Engineers – Conditions of Contract for Building and Engineering works designed by the Employer

14. Hungary

In recent years, FIDIC and FIDIC-based construction contracts have become more common and are now quite widely used, especially for construction works awarded through a tender and/or public procurement.

The form of construction contract to be used is based on the parties' agreement. However, in certain cases, such as public procurement-based construction projects, the use of a standard form contract may be required by the employer.

15. India

In India, any kind of Contract can be executed provided it fulfills the essentials under Indian Contract Act. Therefore, the Standard forms of Contracts in general keep an equal position in the Indian scenario.

16. Ireland

The Royal Institute of Architects in Ireland (in conjunction with the Construction Industry Federation and the Society of Chartered Surveyors) produces the most commonly used forms of building contract, known as the "RIAI forms of contract." The Construction Industry Federation and the Subcontractors and Specialists Association publish the subcontract form. Engineers Ireland (in conjunction with the Association of Consulting Engineers of Ireland) produces the most commonly used engineering contract forms, known as I.E.I. forms of Contract. Government forms of Contract (GC, formerly GDLA) are now generally used for government construction projects or contracts entered into by public bodies. International contract conditions are occasionally used and amended on more considerable project work, including FIDIC, N.E.C., and J.C.T. The state construction contract form depends on the nature of the results, the contracting parties, and the parties' familiarity with the various forms of Contract. For larger construction projects, contracting entities often use standard amended documents drafted and negotiated by in-house lawyers or external counsel. Typically, the party procuring the work (i.e., the land owner or land developer) selects the form of the Contract.

17. Italy

No construction organization typically produces standard contracts for construction projects. However, International Federation of

Consulting Engineers (Fédération Internationale Des Ingénieurs-Conseils) (FIDIC) standard forms can be used for projects in Italy (even if this is not the standard approach), subject to proper adjustments of the relevant text to make it compliant with the Italian legislation and market practice. Two common forms of construction contracts are recognized.

a) A D&B contract is a construction project system where a single entity acts as both designer and builder.

b) Construction contract is usually used by parties intending to undertake civil construction works. Under this structure, the scope of work of the contractor is limited to the preparation of shop drawings and carrying out the construction works while the design is prepared in advance by professionals directly appointed by the employer.

18. Japan

A Japanese joint association of contractors ('Contractors Association') prepares standard contract forms for private works. Although using such conditions is not mandatory, in most cases, these forms are, sometimes with several amendments, used by the parties when entering into a construction or engineering contract. There are also commonly used standard contract forms that the MLIT (Ministry of Land, Infrastructure, Transport and Tourism) prepares for public works. Using any international contract form for Construction in Japan is rare.

19. Kenya

The contracts in use in Kenya, but not limited to FIDIC; World Bank / AfDB Contract; JBCC (Joint Building and Construction Council – formerly Joint Building Council (J.B.C.) contracts; PPOA building contract for Government and Public Works; Agreement and Conditions of Contract for small construction works; Design and Build custom contracts. These documents and other alternatives are available from professional organizations in the Kenyan construction industry.

20. Malawi

International contracts such as FIDIC and N.E.C. are commonly used in large-scale projects. Some locally structured agreements may be available, or contracts from neighboring territories may be used.

21. Mauritius

In the public sector, the most commonly used form of Contract is the General Conditions of Contract (G.C.C.) developed by the Public Procurement Office (P.P.O.) for all scales of projects.

For large-scale projects, P.P.O. allows international standard forms such as FIDIC and the World Bank Standard Conditions of Contract. FIDIC conditions of Contract are the most commonly used in the private sector.

The CIDB Conditions of Contract for Minor Works developed by the Construction Industry Development Board (the local regulator for the construction industry) is often used on small-scale projects. These documents and other alternatives are available from professional organizations in the Mauritian construction industry.

22. Mozambique

International contracts such as FIDIC and New Engineering Contract (N.E.C.) are commonly used in large-scale projects. Some locally structured agreements may be available, or contracts from neighboring territories may be used.

23. Namibia

International contracts such as FIDIC and N.E.C. are commonly used in large-scale projects. Documents used in South Africa are widely used locally, including the JBCC suite of contract documentation in the building sector and the General Conditions of Contract (G.C.C.) for the engineering sector. These documents and other alternatives are available from professional organizations in the S.A. construction industry.

24. Netherlands

In general, Dutch construction law does not require that contracts be standardized. General conditions are often declared applicable to the agreements. These general conditions are often uniform or standardized. The relationship between client and contractor is usually made subject to the following general requirements:

- Uniform Administrative Conditions for the Execution of Works 2012 (Uniforme Administratieve Voorwaarden 2012 (UAV 2012));
- Uniform Administrative Conditions for the Execution of Works for Integrated Forms of Contracts (Uniforme Administratieve Voorwaarden voor Geïntegreerde contractvormen (UAV-GC 2005));
- International forms of contract, like the FIDIC (Fédération Internationale Des Ingénieurs-Conseils) models are also used for more extensive works.
- The relationship between client and architect or structural engineer is often subject to the following general conditions:
- The New Regulations 2011 (De Nieuwe Regeling 2011 (DNR 2011)); and
- Regulations Governing the Relationship between Principals and Consulting Engineers 2001 (Regeling van de Verhouding tussen Opdrachtgever en advisorend Ingenieursbureau 2001 (RVOI 2001)

25. Nigeria

Standard-form contracts are often used in the construction industry in Nigeria. The forms may be amended depending on the requirements of individual projects. Still, the choice of the particular standard form contract depends on the project's size, complexity, and nature.

The standard form contracts used in the Nigerian Construction Industry include the following:

- The International Federation of Consulting Contracts Engineers Forms (the FIDIC Books) is the most common forms with the specific form used, depending on risks allocation and contract structure
- The Standard form of Building Contract in Nigerian 1990 (SFBCN)
- The General Conditions of Contract for the procurement of works, 2011 (the GCC)
- The Joint Contract Tribunal Standard form of Contract (JCT) 2005, and
- Federal Ministry of Works Contract (variant of the JCT)

While International developers do use contract forms such as FIDIC and N.E.C., primary locally structured agreements are commonly used, including the Nigerian Construction Industry for Building Projects Design and Build Articles of Agreement and Conditions of Contract (2018), as well as The Nigerian Construction Industry Articles of Agreement and Conditions of Contract for Building Projects (2018). These documents and other alternatives are available from professional organizations in the Nigerian construction industry.

26. Norway

Several organizations representing contractors and clients cooperate to develop general contract terms incorporated in the industry standard documents. International legal documents, including FIDIC, are seldom used.

27. Poland

In Poland, industry bodies, organizations, or associations don't produce standard form contracts for use within the Construction and engineering sectors.

Generally, the parties' negotiations create construction contracts without legal forms. Concerning international conditions of Contract (such as FIDIC), such documents are sometimes used in investments with high capital expenditure and involving foreign parties. Otherwise, global forms of contracts are rarely used in Poland.

28. Portugal

For public works, the public sector must use a standard form of contract that accords with the provisions of the Public Contracts Code. For private jobs, the parties have to use a legal form of contract that accords with the requirements of the Civil Code and, in addition, with the Public Contracts Code about specific matters (e.g., price, additional works, etc.). FIDIC forms are only used by major contractors or on international contracts.

29. Romania

In Romania, there are no standard contracts provided by the law which must be used in the construction and engineering sectors. However, international forms are often used. FIDIC arrangements are the most frequently used:

- **The Red FIDIC** – Conditions of Contract for Building and Engineering works designed by the Employer

- **The Yellow FIDIC** – Conditions of Contract for Electrical and Mechanical Works and for Building Works designed by the Contractor

30. Rwanda

International contracts such as FIDIC and NEC are used occasionally, mainly in large-scale projects. Locally structured agreements have been developed, including the Rwandan Government RPPDA contract for most small and large projects.

The local practice is to permit lending organizations to determine documentation requirements. These documents and other alternatives are available locally.

31. Slovak Republic

The provisions of the Commercial Code concerning work contracts are mostly non-mandatory, so parties are free to contract. Based on experience, construction companies have evolved the standard form contracts they rely on.

International forms of Contract prepared by FIDIC are becoming increasingly relevant in Slovakia, although they have yet to be adopted in statute. The ideas of FIDIC are being promoted by an interest association of legal entities called the Slovak Association of Consulting Engineers.

32. South Africa

International contracts such as FIDIC and NEC are commonly used in large-scale projects. Numerous locally structured agreements have been developed, including the JBCC suite of contract documentation in the building sector and the General Conditions of Contract (G.C.C.) for the engineering sector.

These documents and other alternatives are available from professional organizations in the S.A. construction industry.

33. Spain

There is no standard contract form in Spain for construction projects. International documents of agreement, such as FIDIC contracts, are still rarely used in Spain, and mainly in projects where they are a requirement when international financing is involved.

34. Sweden

An association called the Construction Contracts Committee (*Byggandets Kontraktskommitté*) prescribes three main standard form contracts:

- **General Conditions for Contracts** – AB 04 is intended for contracts where the employer is responsible for planning and design and the contractor is responsible for the execution
- **General Conditions for Contracts** – ABT 06 is written for turnkey contracts where the contractor is responsible to the employer for both design work and execution
- **General Rules of Agreement for Architectural and Engineering Consulting Services** – ABK 09 is intended to be used for assignments falling within the fields of professional competence of architects and consulting engineers.

International forms of contract, such as FIDIC, are rarely used in Sweden.

35. Tanzania

International contracts such as FIDIC and World Bank are commonly used in large-scale projects. Numerous locally structured agreements have been developed, including the Public Procurement Regulatory Authority (PPRA forms), National Construction Council (NCC / TIQS forms), A.D.B. (African Development Bank), and BADEA conditions of Contract.

These documents and other alternatives are available from professional organizations in the S.A. construction industry.

36. Thailand

For public procurement, the standard agreement under the Regulation of the Ministry of Finance On Public Procurement and Supplies Administration Act, B.E. 2560 (2017), generally applies to any construction contract made with governmental bodies. In the public procurement scheme, the contractor is usually kept from changing or adjusting the significant terms and conditions of the standard agreement.

In cases where the changes in material terms and conditions under the legal contract are necessary, approval from the Office of the Attorney General is required. Concerning a private scheme, although various organizations have produced standard agreements, parties may enter into construction contracts under definitive agreements or otherwise.

The parties' intentions govern the duties and liabilities between the contracting parties, which are subsequently reflected in the terms and conditions of the construction contract.

37. Uganda

International contract forms such as FIDIC, World Bank (IBRD), African Development Bank (A.D.B.), E.U. Form of Contract, U.S. Government Forms of Contract, and Islamic Development Bank contract are commonly used where appropriate.

Numerous locally structured agreements have been developed, including the East African Institute of Architects (EAIA Blue Book) and the Government of Uganda form of Contract (PPDA). These documents and other alternatives are available from professional organizations in the S.A. construction industry.

38. United Arab Emirates - Abu Dhabi

The most popular standard forms of construction contract are from FIDIC. Consultancy contracts tend to be bespoke forms. Abu Dhabi's Procurement Law provides that where government departments are procuring construction and engineering services, standard documents issued by the government, based on FIDIC contracts, are to be used.

39. United Arab Emirates - Dubai

No local standard suite of construction contracts is used in Dubai. Generally, the Dubai construction market has used an amended FIDIC style of Contract; however, other forms of bespoke agreements are used, depending on the size and nature of the deal.

40. UK - England and Wales

In the U.K., standard form building contracts go back more than one hundred years. Initial collaboration between the Royal Institute of British Architects (RIBA) and the then federation of construction employers led to the first standard form of building contract. These bodies subsequently formed the Joint Contracts Tribunal (J.C.T.), now the main U.K. body that produces legal form contracts, guidance notes, and other documentation for use in the construction industry. The main rival to the J.C.T family of contracts is the NEC and its suite of Engineering and Construction Contracts (E.C.C.), endorsed by the U.K. Government. It is now being used more in government contracting. Some of the leading professional bodies that govern the activities of construction consultants and also produce contracts for the appointment of their members to provide design and consultancy services are as below:

- **Royal Institute of British Architects (RIBA)** – architects
- **Institution of Civil Engineers (ICE)** – civil engineers
- **Institution of Mechanical Engineers (IMechE)** – mechanical engineers
- **Institution of Engineering and Technology (IET)** – electrical engineers
- **Association for Consultancy and Engineering (ACE)** – all types of engineer involved in building projects
- **Institution of Chemical Engineers (IChemE)** – chemical and process engineers and material scientists
- **Royal Institute of Chartered Surveyors (RICS)** – quantity surveyors
- **Association for Project Safety (APS)** – health and safety consultants

International forms of contract (such as FIDIC) are rarely used in the UK.

41. UK - Scotland

In the U.K., standard form building contracts go back more than one hundred years. Initial collaboration between the Royal Institute of British Architects (RIBA) and the then federation of construction employers led to the first standard form of building contract. These bodies subsequently formed the Joint Contracts Tribunal (J.C.T.), now the main U.K. body that produces legal form contracts, guidance notes, and other documentation for use in the construction industry. In Scotland, the Scottish Building Contracts Committee (SBCC) adapts and publishes Scots law-compliant versions of the J.C.T. suite of contracts. The latest edition of these contracts was published in 2016. The main rival to the JCT/SBCC family of contracts is the NEC and its suite of Engineering and Construction Contracts (E.C.C.) published by the Institution of Civil Engineers.

The U.K. and Scottish governments have endorsed this, and are now widely used in government contracting. The latest edition of these contracts (NEC4) was published in June 2017. The leading professional bodies that govern the activities of construction consultants also produce contracts for the appointment of their members to provide design and consultancy services, namely:

- **Royal Incorporation of Architects in Scotland (RIAS)** – architects
- **Institution of Civil Engineers (ICE)** – civil & structural engineers
- **Institution of Mechanical Engineers (IMechE)** – mechanical engineers
- **Institution of Engineering and Technology (IET)** – electrical engineers
- **Association of Consulting Engineers (ACE)** – all types of engineer involved in building projects
- **Institution of Chemical Engineers (IChemE)** – chemical and process engineers and material scientists
- **Royal Institution of Chartered Surveyors in Scotland** – quantity surveyors
- **The Association for Project Safety (APS)** – health and safety consultants.

International forms of contract (such as FIDIC) are also used in the UK, typically in the infrastructure and energy sectors. The latest edition of the FIDIC contracts was published in 2017 (although modified 1999 versions are more widely used in the UK, as the 2017 versions are less popular with developers and funders).

42. Zambia

International contracts such as FIDIC and New Engineering Contract (NEC) are commonly used in large-scale projects. Some locally structured agreements may be available, or forms from neighboring territories may be used.

43. Zimbabwe

The Construction Industry Federation of Zimbabwe (CIFoZ) is the construction industry association, and it has established the National Joint Practice Committee (NJPC) Standard Contracts 2000. These contracts are based on FIDIC Contracts and have been approved by FIDIC.

In short, as an individual or as an organization, you should review your existing and upcoming contract agreements and evaluate the possibility of using standard forms of contracts to ease and expedite the whole process of creating contract agreements. In the next chapter, we will examine the terms and conditions of a significant construction contract using the FIDIC Red book, 1999, as a standard form of contract.

Call to Action:
You are requested to review the standard forms of contracts being used in your industry or geography. You are welcome to share your thoughts on the same on **www.prasamviidah.com** or write to manish.mohandas@outlook.com

CHAPTER 4:

FIDIC RED BOOK 1999 – A CLOSER LOOK

Now that we have seen the various options of standard forms of contract available for use and to explore further, let us examine one of these standard forms of contract and understand each part of the conditions and its implications. For the purpose of discussions here, I would prefer to use the FIDIC red book (1999) as the standard form of contract. This is being used purely due to the familiarity of its use in the construction industry. The concepts that we discuss here can also be used for other forms of contract.

The FIDIC 1999 (Red book) is a standard form of contract used in construction projects where the project is designed by the Employer (also known as the Client) and constructed by the Contractor. A copy of the FIDIC 1999 book can be obtained from the publications section at www.fidic.org. I will provide an overview of its contents and we can discuss the conditions in details. The FIDIC 1999 (Red book) contains 20 main clauses/sections which are further subdivided into sub sections. I will attempt to discuss each subsection in brief.

Source: www.fidic.org

Section 1 – General Provisions

The general provisions cover various topics such as:

i. Definitions: There are various words used within the contract agreement, such as Employer, Contractor, Site, Works etc. The exact meanings of these definitions have to be clearly mentioned with the Contract. In case the definitions provided in the standard form of contract does not protect the interests of one of the parties, then this condition has to be negotiated and modified accordingly. For example, the definition of the Employer or the Contractor means a particular organization which on a particular date is represented by the Owners or Directors of that organization. Does the definition cover what happens if the Owners are either no more (not alive) or the current owners have sold their company to some other person or company? If Bob as a buyer decides to sell his house and property mid-way through construction to someone else, where does that leave the Contractor? Will the contractor get his payments from Bob or from the new company? Will the new owner of the house be obligated to continue this contract? What happens to the contractor's investments made with the assumption that he will be constructing this house and receiving agreed sums of money? What happens to Bob if a similar and a vice versa situation is applied to the Contractor's organization? Will the new owner of the contracting organization be obligated to continue constructing Bob's house or will Bob be required to carry out the whole tendering process again? Does the Employer or Contractor imply that their Legal heirs, successors etc. are also bound by the Contract agreement? This would need to be discussed and negotiated. There is usually a clause relating to assignment which is covered in every contract agreement. This means whether parties to any contract agreement have the right to assign these contracts to any other person or organization and if so, what are the conditions under which the same can be done. The definitions section in any contract needs to be understood by all parties to the Contract.

ii. Interpretation, communications: These terms clarify whether the communications have to be specifically done in a pre-agreed manner. For example, whether WhatsApp or other forms of social media communications are an agreed and acceptable form of communication between the parties or are there are restrictions? Would the stakeholders have to communicate using a particular portal or intranet? Or would the stakeholders have to communicate using physical copies of letters or would it be sufficient to communicate over emails?

iii. Law and Language: This section specifies the agreed language of communication. It also states the applicability of law. For example, if there is a contract agreement between two parties from two different countries, it is best to specify the laws of which country will be followed by the Parties in the event of a dispute. Further, it would be in the interest of all parties to a contract to state which language shall override in case of a possible difference in interpretations between two languages.

iv. Priority of Documents: A contract agreement usually has multiple sections and annexures that form part of the whole document. It is possible that in some cases, there could be some contradiction or ambiguity created due to the details available in 2 or 3 different sections of the Contract agreement. In such cases, which one supersedes? The condition pertaining to priority of documents specifies this aspect. For example, in a construction contract, there are drawings, specifications and say a document called the Bill of quantities (BOQ). Let us say that the drawings mention that a door has to be 2.1 meters high whereas in the specifications document, the same door is mentioned as having a requirement of say 2.2 meters high. Now which is the correct reference based on which the Contractor would have priced his bid. In case the priority of documents state that the specifications document has a higher priority over the drawings, then the door would need to be 2.2 meters high. Of course, the Client may change the requirement and the same may be considered as a variation to the contract agreement. For complex projects, the priority of documents may have to be carefully reviewed and incorporated within the contract agreement.

v. There are other sections such as use of documents provided by other party, confidentiality conditions, joint and several liability etc.

Section 2 – The Employer

This section covers various aspects such as:

i. Access to the Working Areas: This sub section specifies the party responsible for providing the access to the working area, the time period within which it need to be provided and the manner in which the access is provided.

ii. Permits, licenses and approvals: This subsection specifies the responsibilities of the parties in matters relating to obtaining various permits, licenses, approvals etc., for the project. This is a very important aspect. In case the contractor constructs a house and is unable to get the necessary approvals at the end of the construction, then all efforts spent on the project could go waste. Usually, such approvals are withheld by the government authorities due to non-adherence to some statute. Hence depending on whose responsibility this is, it is an aspect that need to be discussed and detailed out. There could be various types of approvals and it is possible that the responsibilities could be shared between the parties depending on who is best placed to obtain it based on competence. In construction projects, most of the permits are usually obtained by the Employer/Client. However, it could vary based on specific project requirements.

iii. Employer's Personnel: The Employer's personnel may need to be defined especially if the Employer is a large organization as there could be multiple stakeholders from the Employer's organization who may be involved at various stages of a project. In such cases it may be best to agree and define that employer's personnel could mean a specific set of employees or any other third party employed by the Employer.

iv. **Employer's Financial Arrangements**: Some of the standard conditions of contract provide for this condition. Though this could be a very sensitive aspect to discuss from the point of view of the contractor, it is in the best interest of everyone involved to agree on this condition. For example, at some stage during the construction of the project, it may be possible that the Contractor observes some challenges in funding being faced by the Employer. In such a situation, if this is a pre agreed condition, the Contractor may request the Employer to furnish details of the Employer's financial arrangements to satisfy that the Contractor can proceed with the completion of the Project without any concerns of financial default by the employer.

Section 3 – The Engineer

Now in major contracts, sometimes the parties agree to include a third-party professional organization to act as a neutral party in administering the said contract agreement. Such a party is referred to as the Engineer in FIDIC forms of Contract. This may not be applicable if the parties agree for the same. Another important aspect that may need to be clearly mentioned is that if this third-party organization need to be changed midway through the construction of this project, what would the terms and conditions and would this change need to be approved by some or all the stakeholders?

Section 4 – The Contractor

In construction contracts, the contractor has multiple obligations. It is in the interest of all stakeholders to define this clearly within the contract agreement. Some of the major ones are list below:

i. **General obligations**: Under this section, the Contractor's general obligations are usually specified. Such obligations could include the extent to which the contractor carries project design responsibility, the amount of plant and machinery that the Contractor would deploy at the construction site and the duration for the same, the contractor's responsibility in relation to the adequacy, stability and safety of construction, the methods by which the contractor intends to construct the works etc.

ii. **Performance security**: In construction contracts, it is a usual industry practice for the contractor to provide some form of security to the client. This security is an assurance for the client that the contractor would definitely complete the construction project within the agreed terms and conditions. Usually, such security is provided in the form of bank guarantees or such other forms as may be agreed between the parties. The value of performance security is usually defined as a percentage of the contract value and is agreed at the time of signing the contract agreement. This security is usually in addition to any other securities which the contractor may require to provide for in return for any advance amounts which the Employer may provide to the Contractor in order for the contractor to mobilize his resources.

iii. **Contractor's representative**: Similar to the Employer's personnel, the Contractor's representative also needs to be well defined within the Contract agreement. The Contract agreement must insist for an appropriate documentation on who would represent the Contractor in various matters. It could also specify the process of notification in case the particular individual is required to be changed due to various reasons.

iv. **Sub-contracting**: The Client/Employer may have selected a particular contractor considering their credentials and competency and may have actually agreed special terms and a premium to avail their services. Now what happens if the selected contractor decides to sublet the entire work to another contractor (usually called as a sub-contractor) for commercial gains? Where does it leave the Client in terms of quality assurance? Hence this is the condition where the parties would need to mutually agree the extent to which the contractor is allowed to sub contract certain parts of the works. There could also be certain works or services which the client would like the contractor to procure from selected and specified suppliers. The names of these suppliers would need to be specified within the contract agreement. In case the contractor wishes to sub contract a portion of the works in addition to what was agreed within the contract agreement, then the contractor would need to obtain a specific approval from the Client stating reasons why they wish to do so. The Client after reviewing such reasons may approve or reject such requests. However, it is important to review this aspect at the time of signing the contract agreement.

v. **Quality and safety assurance:** In order to ensure that the works are carried out in line with the agreed quality parameters, the client may want the contractor to set a detailed quality assurance system. Similarly, the contractor is expected to adhere to safe work practices to ensure that the works are carried out in a safe manner.

vi. **Site data:** This is a condition which need to be satisfied by both parties. For example, the Buyer would need to provide specific details about the location of the site where the works have to be carried out. In case of construction an example could be the condition of the site below ground level. This is usually understood by carrying out certain sub soil investigations. Such reports are usually shared with the Contractor in order for them to plan their works. Now the Contractor is at liberty to independently carry out such studies. Whether the contractor would be compensated for carrying out such studies or not is something which would be specified in the section titled "Instruction to Bidders" in the Bid/Tender document. The Contractor would also be expected to satisfy other factors such as climatic conditions, any restrictions of working hours, local laws and practices, holidays, festivals, accommodation facilities for workmen, sanitary facilities for workmen both at the place of residence as well as the place of work, transport arrangements, messing facilities and any other relevant parameter that would have an effect on the works.

vii. **Rights of way and facilities:** The Contractor is expected to make all arrangements to create access facilities for carrying out works. If the contractor expects the employer to make some arrangements, then the same shall be negotiated and agreed in the contract agreement. Further if there is a requirement to create any special facilities outside the construction site, then the terms and conditions for the same have to be discussed and negotiated in the contract agreement. For example, in large construction projects like construction of a bridge, it is possible that the contractor may need some space away from the actual bridge site. The space is required by the contractor to fabricate certain components (such as pre cast bridge parts) of the construction and then bring it to the construction site to assemble the same. Parameters such as who will procure or lease this space/land, who will pay for it, for how long will this space be needed etc. will need to be discussed and agreed at the beginning and captured accordingly within the contract agreement.

viii. **Avoidance of interference:** While carrying out works, it is important for all stakeholders involved to avoid or minimize any interference with public facilities. If there is an unavoidable situation, the parties are expected to take necessary approvals etc as needed to carry out such works with minimum interference to any public facility (e.g traffic). The responsibilities in this regard may be discussed and agreed and captured appropriately within the Contract Agreement.

ix. **Employer's free issued materials:** In some contracts, it is possible that for various operational or commercial reasons the Employer or Client or the Buyer may want to buy certain items and provide it to the Contractor on a free of cost basis. The Contractor may have a certain scope of installing such items which is provided free of cost to the Contractor. An example could be if Bob wishes to buy a premium variety of bathroom fittings which he wants the contractor to only install in the bathroom. Now the reason why Bob may want to do this is many. For example, Bob has a liking for a certain product from a particular brand and he wants to ensure that this requirement is not compromised by the Contractor. Perhaps Bob is in a better position to negotiate with supplier of this product and hence he stands to get a better price.

x. **Site security:** This condition specifies who would be responsible for the security of the construction site. It is possible in construction contracts that the Employer/Buyer may employ multiple contractors at the same time to carry out various trades of works. In such a case, it may be in the best interest of the Employer to either retain site security as one of his responsibilities or instruct one of the major contractors on the site to be responsible for it. However, in case of Bob, since there is only one contractor constructing his dream house, it would be better to let the contractor manage the security till such time that the construction works are in progress.

xi. Fossils: In construction contracts it is possible that while carrying out the underground works, the contractor may discover/recover some fossils or other materials of historical significance. It is recommended to include a provision within your contract agreements for such events. For example, in case such items are found then the same may be handed over to the Employer or Owner of the land. Depending on the country in which such works are being carried out, it may be expected of the citizens to handover such items to the relevant government authorities.

Section 5 – Nominated Sub-Contractor

While carrying out specific works, the Employer may require the Contractor to avail services from a particular organization for multiple reasons, and this could be a condition under the specific contract. For example, while constructing a multistoried building, it is possible that the Employer wishes that the Contractor use a particular brand of elevators in the building. This may be due to commitments to customers, marketing compulsions, or just an employer's preference for a certain brand or product. Now, unlike the materials, which are issued free of cost, as discussed in section 4, this service cannot be issued free of cost as it may involve detailed engineering, procurement, installation, testing, and commissioning. Hence, it is best to be executed by the Contractor. In such cases, the Employer may nominate such specialized service providers to the Contractor. The Contractor is usually paid a fee over and above the fees paid to the specialized service provider for any support that this Contractor may be required to provide. If the Contractor has reasons (and evidence) to believe that such "Employer nominated specialized contractor" does not have the capability or the resources to carry out such specialized works, then the Contractor may object to such nomination. If the Contractor has no objection to such nomination, then the Contractor is expected to place orders to such "Employer nominated specialized contractor" and carry out works as any other sub-contractor employed by the Contractor. As the employer has nominated the specialized Contractor, the employer may want to see evidence of timely payments being made by the Contractor to the "Employer nominated specialized contractor." Similarly, the Contractor may make the payments to the "Employer nominated specialized contractor" only upon receiving corresponding payments from the Employer. These conditions may have to be discussed and captured appropriately within the contract agreement.

Section 6 – Staff and Labor

The contractor is expected to employ staff and labor for carrying out the construction. In this regard, it is best to discuss, agree and specify certain conditions within the contract agreement:

i. The contractor shall pay wages to their staff and labor in line with the minimum wages as approved by the government for that geography. In addition to satisfying the minimum wage criteria, the wages may also be required to align with those paid in the industry. This is in the best interest of the Contractor. This condition has to be specified in the Tender document itself because it prevents any unfair attempts at cost-cutting by the Contractor after the works have been awarded to them. Similarly, it presents any unfair requests for discounts on this account by the employer while carrying out negotiations.

ii. During the tenure of the contract, it may be discussed and agreed that neither party will recruit any staff from the other party. This is to protect the interests of both parties. However, this may be evaluated in line with any existing laws of the specific country.

iii. **Labor Laws:** Each country has their own labor laws. These could cover various aspects such as medical insurance, provident fund, immigration requirements, interstate migration rules etc.

An exhaustive list of such labor laws which are currently applicable in India are available in www.prasamviidah.com.

iv. **Working Hours**: Every geographic location has prevalent practices with respect to weekly days off, festival holidays, and practices related to local customs. Both parties are expected to honor these practices, and the same would need to be discussed and captured in the contract agreement. For example, the usual working hours in a location would be 9 am to 5 pm. However, in construction projects, at times, due to operational reasons, the working hours for a particular day could extend beyond usual working hours. This is a deviation from the prevalent practices. If the work demands a deviation from any of these practices, then the arrangements in such cases would need to be discussed and captured in the contract agreement. For example, the workers may need to be compensated for overtime labor at higher rates. In addition, some facilities like food and lodging may have to be arranged for the period of deviation.

v. **Facilities for Staff and Labor**: In the case of small works spread over shorter durations, the workers of the employer and the contractor may arrange for their own food and accommodation. However, if the project being undertaken is complex, in a remote location and spread over an extended duration, it would be best to consider various aspects such as the construction of living quarters, messing facilities, and entertainment facilities.

Section 7 - Plant, Materials and Workmanship

This section pertains to aspects such as:

i. The manner in which works need to be executed.

ii. The requirement for the contractor to submit any samples for the employer's approval (e.g., samples of finishing materials such as tiles, marble, etc.)

iii. The requirement for the contractor to allow full access to the employer or any other stakeholder for carrying out inspection during and after the completion of the construction activities.

iv. The requirements for carrying out testing of materials or works, the apparatus required for the same, the methods, timing, frequency of carrying out such tests, insights on whether or not these tests need to be carried out at the construction site or any other external third-party location, and which party bears the costs associated with such testing

v. The steps to be taken by the contractor and the employer in case of rejection of any material or works, remedial actions to be taken and who bears the costs for the same.

vi. **The Royalties to be paid under the Contract**

It can be noted that some of the above conditions may not even apply to certain works. However, it is in the interest of all stakeholders to review the above conditions and specifically incorporate whatever is agreed upon between the Parties. If the parties think that some aspect does not apply to a particular contract, then it is better to mention the condition and state that it does not apply. For e.g., in some projects, there may not be a requirement for submitting samples. Hence, it could be specifically mentioned that there is no requirement for submission of samples under this contract.

Section 8 – Commencement, Delays, and Suspension

This section relates to the aspect of time for the scope of works under the contract agreement. It covers aspects such as:

i.Commencement of Work: As we all know; every project has a commencement date (more commonly known as a Start date) and a completion date. In complex construction projects, what could be considered a commencement date? There could be multiple activities to be completed before a commencement date can be established. For example, the contractor may need the construction site to be handed over free of any hurdles, the necessary drawings approved by the authorities for the initial part of the works, some advance payments, if agreed under the contract, and perhaps some other relevant and dependent activity. If any of these activities are delayed, the commencement date gets delayed. Hence, in order to avoid any disagreements at a later date, it is in the interest of all stakeholders to agree to the activities that would determine the commencement date.

ii. **Time for Completion**: There are two stages in construction contracts. Stage 1 is when the works have been completed, the constructed facility has been taken over by the employer, and perhaps the employer has commenced the use of the facility. Stage 2 is usually the completion of what is known as the defects notification period. The defects notification period usually ranges from 12 months to 24 months from the completion of stage 1 and is specified to provide an opportunity for the employer to identify any possible defects that may have come to light during the use of the facility by the employer. The contractor also gets an opportunity to correct the defects during this defects notification period. So, the contract is strictly complete only when the defects notification period is completed. In construction contracts, completion of stage 1 is usually documented by the issue of a Taking-over certificate or Virtual completion certificate. The completion of stage 2 is usually documented by the issuance of a performance certificate.

iii. **Program**: Apart from the commencement date and the time for completion, it is important for all stakeholders to agree on the sequence and methods in which the work will be carried out. It is recommended to have interim milestones within the contract agreement to ensure that the works are progressing at the expected rate of progress. In the event the milestones are not being met, the stakeholders get an early warning to take corrective actions to ensure that the contract completion is not delayed.

iv. **Extension of Time**: It is recommended to agree with the conditions under which the extension of time may be permitted under the contract. In some cases, it may not be possible to provide an extension of time. For example, in some geographies, there may be a requirement to complete certain works before the onset of winter or monsoon, which may have a tremendous negative impact on the construction. Let us consider a beachfront property where there is a requirement to carry out edge protection before the onset of heavy monsoons. If the edge protection is not carried out before the monsoon, apart from the fact that the works cannot be carried out during monsoon, it is possible that a part of the property may be lost during monsoon. Hence, in such cases, an extension of time cannot be given. However, if the completion of the project can be delayed by some time, then an extension of time may be given. However, the conditions under which such extension of time may be provided could be pre-defined under the contract. Another aspect to consider here is how the extension of time would be addressed in the event of a delay caused by a third party, such as a local authority. It is best to agree to such aspects at the start of the contract.

v. **Delay Damages**: In the interest of clarity, it may be best to agree to the consequences of delay. For example, if a contract is scheduled to be completed in 20 months, then the employer may allow an extension of a maximum of 2 months due to any default by the contractor with a certain rate of delay penalty per week of delay, subject to some upper limit. If the expectations are defined in the contract, it reduces the chances of any disagreements at a later date.

vi. **Suspension of Work**: The parties could also discuss and agree for arrangements to be made in case of any foreseeable or unforeseeable events that may lead to the suspension of works. For example, if the parties anticipate a temporary suspension of work due to some local elections, it could be factored into the contract. Under such conditions, whether an extension of time has to be given or not has to be agreed upon upfront while signing the contract agreement.

Each of the above elements are discussed in details below.

- Clause 8 encompasses essential provisions concerning the commencement of the works, the Time for Completion, delays, and the Contractor's entitlement to an extension of time. It also addresses the Employer's right to claim delay damages. Additionally, it specifies the circumstances leading to a suspension of the Works and the implications for both Parties. The "Commencement of Work Sub-Clause" specifies when construction works will begin. The conditions require the Employer to give the Contractor not less than seven days' notice of the Commencement Date. Unless otherwise provided, the Commencement Date must be within 42 days of the Letter of Acceptance. Thereafter, the Contractor must commence as soon as reasonably practicable. 'Works' are defined narrowly and mean Permanent and Temporary works, and it is this which must be started as soon as reasonably possible. The definitions of 'Contractor's Equipment' and 'Temporary Works' support the view that the 'Works' may not cover all aspects of mobilization. However, the definition of 'Temporary Works' would cover the setting up of the site camp, laboratories, etc. If the Employer fails to give notice of the Commencement Date, such an act could be a breach of contract, and the Contractor might be entitled to claim an extension of time and costs. The Commencement of Works must be read together with the clause that relates to the Right of Access to the Site. Access for the Contractor must be given from commencement. If no time is prescribed, then the Employer must make sure that such parts of the

Site are made available so that the Contractor can pursue the intended sequence and methods he set out in the Program. It should be noted that in many instances, there will be no need for the Contractor to have access to all parts of the Site at once. Failure to give access to the Site would no doubt trigger a claim for an extension of time and costs. Furthermore, it is recommended that the requirements of the Contract be seen in relation to the Rate of Progress. This goes beyond simply starting and maintaining work; it entails progressing in line with the Contractor's submitted plans and resources, particularly when this alignment is crucial for completing the project. To determine if the Contractor is progressing at the appropriate rate, the updated program, is used as the benchmark. In this relation, it is also recommended to see the particular obligations of the Contractor to provide updated programs under the Contract. Time for Completion is the Contractor's paramount time-related obligation; he must complete the whole of the Works and, if applicable, each Section of the Works within the time required by the Contract, subject to any extensions of time to which he may be entitled. The time within which the Works must be completed is calculated from the Commencement Date. The Contract may refer to the 'whole of the Works,' which means the passing of Tests on Completion and all work required to be completed for the purposes of issuing a Taking-Over Certificate, except for minor outstanding works and defects which may not substantially affect the use of the Works or their intended purpose. The Contractor is required to provide a detailed Program within a certain timeline (usually 28 days of the receipt of the Notice of Commencement.) It is to be revised whenever it is inconsistent with actual progress or the Contractor's obligations. The Contract may include a requirement for the Contractor to provide details as to timing and methods that must be included in the

Program, and this will make it easier to identify when there has been a breach of this condition. One might consider that an Employer may not be concerned about methods and timing provided the end result is supplied on time. However, it is recommended that both Parties include these in the Contract for later reference. The Employer will want to be able to rely on it for the purposes of giving possession of the Site. Failure to give possession of the Site may provide the Contractor entitlement to an extension of time and Cost. The Contractor may also be required to give notice of probable future events which may adversely affect or delay the actual execution of the Works. This means any event, not just events that may affect the contractual Time for Completion. While it is no doubt good practice for the Contractor in any event to revise or update his Program, he may now be expressly required to revise it;

- Whenever the current Program is inconsistent with actual progress or with his obligations or,
- In the event that he gives notice of specific probable future events or circumstances which may adversely affect or delay the execution of the Works, or
- If the Employer gives him notice that the Program fails to comply either with the Contract or is inconsistent with actual progress and the Contractor's stated intentions.

Extension of Time for Completion: This condition sets out the mechanism by which an extension of the Time for Completion may be determined. The starting point is that any delay must affect the completion of the Works. Therefore, a distinction is made between non-critical delays and critical delays. Critical delays may possibly give an entitlement to an extension of time. The Contractor must comply with the appropriate procedure. For example, the words' if and to the extent that completion is or will be delayed by...' make it clear that it is a delay to completion as provided for in the Contract, which is to be compensated for by the extension of time and not merely disruption to progress attributable to any cause. Each of the possible causes listed is detailed below: -

a) A 'Variation' or 'other substantial change in the quantity of an item of work. Variations may include changes to quantities, omission of any work, any additional work, plant, materials, or services, and changes to the sequence and timing of the Works. The changes to the sequence and timing of the Works have become more significant in light of the rigorous requirements for the Program that may have been set out under the Contract. Entitlement to an extension of time elsewhere in the Conditions can be due to the following possible reasons.

b) Delayed Drawings or Instructions from the Employer may allow for Extension of time, Cost and reasonable profit

c) Right of Access to the Site (being delayed by the Employer) may allow for Extension of time, Cost and reasonable profit

d) Setting Out may allow for Extension of time, Cost and reasonable profit

e) Unforeseeable physical conditions (if not provided for appropriately during negotiations and under the Contract) may allow for Extension of time and Cost

f) Fossils may allow for Extension of time and Cost

g) Testing (if specific demands are made by the Employer beyond what is specified in the Contract) may allow for Extension of time, Cost and reasonable profit

h) Extension of time may be allowed due to other causes such as

- Delays caused by authorities may allow for Extension of time

- Consequences of Suspension of works by the Employer may allow for Extension of time and Cost
- Interference (by the Employer) with Tests on Completion may allow for Extension of time, Cost and reasonable profit
- Adjustments for changes in legislation may allow for Extension of time and Cost
- Contractor's entitlement to suspend work may allow Extension of time, Cost and reasonable profit
- Consequences of Employer's risks may allow for Extension of time, Cost and reasonable profit in some instances
- Force Majeure may allow for Extension of time and Cost in some instances
- 'Exceptionally adverse climatic conditions.' The FIDIC Guide suggests that a way of establishing whether such climatic conditions have, in fact, occurred would be to consider the frequency with which similar adverse conditions have occurred at the Site in light of the length of the Contract period. For example, for a two-year contract, conditions that occurred 4 or 5 times the length of the contract period, i.e., once every 8 to 10 years, might be exceptionally adverse. In order to qualify for an extension of time, the climatic conditions must be 'exceptionally adverse.'
- 'Unforeseeable shortages of personnel or Goods caused by epidemic or Governmental actions.' 'Unforeseeable' is defined as 'not reasonably foreseeable by an experienced Contractor by the date for submission of the Tender'. This definition may or may not be applied to the availability of labor or goods.
- 'Any delay, impediment or prevention...' caused by the Employer, his Personnel or other contractors.

Delays Caused by Authorities: This Sub-Clause provides that unforeseeable delay or disruption caused to a Contractor by a public authority may give entitlement to an extension of time

Rate of Progress: This Sub-Clause establishes the framework for the Employer to track progress using the Contractor's submitted Program as outlined in the Contract. It also empowers the Employer to demand that the Contractor, responsible for delays under the Contract, submits a Program detailing how they will accelerate the project to meet the Time for Completion (which is to include any extension of time granted). The Contractor shall adopt the methods described, and the Employer can claim the costs incurred.

Delay Damages: This is the Sub-Clause, which sets out the amount, up to the maximum stated in the Contract, that can be paid by the Contractor to the Employer in the event of late completion of the Works or any Section, if applicable. The Employer may not be entitled to recover his actual losses.

The Contractor knows in advance the likely level of his risk in the event of delay, and the Employer has some certainty as to his recovery levels in the event of delay and avoids the hurdles involved in proving his actual loss. The delay damages could be the only damages due from the Contractor to the Employer for 'such default,' i.e., for the failure to comply with the Time for Completion.

It may expressly exclude liability of the Contractor to the Employer for loss of use of the Works (permanent or temporary) even if that loss of use is caused by the Contractor's failure to comply with the Time for Completion, and otherwise delay damages would be triggered. Upon termination by the Employer, the position could be different.

Suspension of Work, Consequences and Resumption of Work

The Suspension clause empowers the Employer to instruct the Contractor to suspend part or all of the Works. If this occurs, the Contractor must protect the Works against damage. The Employer may inform the Contractor of the reason for the suspension but may be under no obligation to do so. If the suspension is not due to the

Contractor's default, there could be a procedure for the parties to follow, and the same may be set out in the Contract.

In the event of a prolonged suspension, the Contract may allow the Contractor to ask permission to proceed, and if permission is declined, he may notify an omission or may give notice of termination under the Contract.

During suspension, the Contract may require the Contractor to 'protect, store, and secure such part or the Works against any deterioration, loss, or damage.'

Any Cost which the Employer may determine under the Contract would no doubt include the cost of the secure storage of the Works or part of the Works.

The Contractor must comply with the notification requirements as per the Contract when claiming that the instruction to suspend caused him delay and /or Cost. He is required to give notice to the Employer.

- The Contract may provide that a Contractor will not be entitled to recover time or Cost if he is responsible for making good his own faulty design or workmanship or materials, nor his failure to comply with the safe protection provisions. Where the suspension has been for work on Plant or delivery of Plant /Materials for more than a certain period (usually 28 days) and the Plant/Materials have been marked as the Employer's property, the Contract may provide for the Contractor to be paid the value of Plant and Materials which have not been delivered to Site.
- The Contract may provide for what happens in the event of a prolonged suspension; if the suspension has continued for more than a certain period (usually 84 days) then the Contractor may ask for 'permission' to proceed. If the Employer declines to so do within a further period (usually

28 days), the Contractor may notify that the suspension is an omission. If the whole of the Works is affected then the Contractor may terminate the Contract.

Section 9 – Tests on Completion

The conditions relating to testing of works could be:

i.   The obligations of the parties with respect to carrying out the tests need to be discussed and agreed upon. For example, in some cases, there would be an excessive requirement for electricity and water to carry out such tests. It has to be agreed on who would arrange for these resources to carry out such tests. Another example of this could be the witnesses required for carrying out such tests, i.e., who all are required to witness the tests? Further, does the witness have to be physically present at the test location, or considering more recent advanced tools, can this be witnessed remotely?

ii.   In case testing is delayed due to either of the parties, then the arrangements and timelines for the other party to carry out the tests may need to be discussed and agreed upon.

iii.   In case a particular section of work fails to pass the tests, then it would be better to discuss and agree on what the corrective actions would be. There could be multiple options. One option is to re-test the works again. Another option could be to demolish the part and reconstruct the same. However, sometimes, this is not possible due to specific operational reasons. In such cases, one more option would be to use the defective part with some additional reinforcements or rectifications. In such cases, the understanding of the additional costs would need to be pre-agreed between the parties.

Each of the above elements are discussed in details below.

Tests are commonly required for certain contracts after completion.

There may, for example, be a requirement for a specific test during a period of initial functioning. Sometimes, the tests need to be carried out in different seasons of the year to test functioning under various conditions, whether from weather or load. Thus, by definition, the Plant is likely to be under the control of the Employer by the time the Tests are to be carried out. Some standard contracts thus assume that the tests will be carried out by the Employer, although the results will potentially lead to obligations being imposed on the Contractor. There may be an obligation for the Employer's staff who carry out the test to be both competent and able to carry out the tests properly. When these tests are conducted, the corresponding portion of the work will have been finished and be operational. It's evident that tests performed by individuals who do not possess the required qualifications might lack credibility or reliability. This is a serious issue where the Works include complex plants because, at least immediately after the time of taking over, it is quite possible that the Employer's staff (probably those who will eventually run the Plant) may not be sufficiently experienced to meet the requirements. If they are not, they may not be able to operate and thus test it to its required efficiency, and the test results will be misleading. Indeed, if they are the same people who have been running the plant for some time, their lack of competence may have contributed to any shortfall in performance. In the event that the Contractor disagrees with the results and can identify any lack of competence on the part of the Employer's testing team, it will be able to take issue with the results of the Tests. Since the competence of the testing staff is an element of the requirement for testing, the mere fact that the Employer's testing staff does not meet the standard required ought to be a sufficient argument to say that the Employer is not entitled to rely on the tests. This may even be without proving that the plant would, if properly tested, have met the required standards. A further provision may require that the tests be carried out in accordance with the Employer's Requirements and the Operations and Maintenance Manuals. The tests are to be carried out in the presence of the Contractor if the Employer or the

Contractor so requests. There could be a provision enabling the timing of Tests after Completion to be provided for in the Contract and to provide the Contractor with notice of the date and a program for the timing. The Contract may allow for the imposition of Performance Damages or for the Contractor to remedy the non-performance discovered in the tests. The Contract may make it possible for the Employer to bypass the Contractor's right and obligation to remedy defects and simply levy Performance Damages. The Contract may give the Contractor an option to remedy defects. The Contract must be designed to deal with the situation where the Employer is in occupation and operating where the Employer may possibly be entitled to delay access to accommodate its operational requirements.

Failure to pass tests after completion may allow the Contractor to pay any prescribed non-performance damages.

He may then be released from any obligation to remedy the discovered shortfall in performance.

Section 10 – Employer's taking over

Once the testing of the works has been completed and the results are found to be satisfactory, the employer usually takes over the work and starts using it. This is normal practice. However, I wish to draw your attention to a scenario where part of the work is delayed.

For example, for the construction of Bob's two-floor dream house, if the construction of the ground floor was completed, but the first-floor completion was delayed for various reasons, could Bob and his family take over the ground floor and start using it while construction is still in progress on the first floor?

This is an example of partial completion and taking over of the work. It is recommended to discuss this aspect and include the same within the agreement.

Further aspects that need to be considered under the Taking Over of the Works are detailed below.

Taking over the works, sections, or parts of the works.

Taking-over by the Employer happens when the Works:

a) Pass the Tests on Completion;
b) Are substantially complete;
c) Any contractual requirements relating to Taking-Over have been met; and
d) The Taking-Over Certificate has been issued or is deemed to have been issued.

The Contract may have provisions with deemed Taking-Over where the Employer uses part of the Works or interferes with the Tests on Completion for more than a certain period. The failure to issue a Taking-Over Certificate by the Employer, where the Employer has taken into commercial use the Works, will amount to a breach of Contract.

Employer's obligation of Taking-Over of the Works– This condition applies except in case of failure to Pass Tests on Completion. Therefore, if the Works pass the Tests on Completion, the Employer shall Take-Over the Works (or a Section, if any) when:

i.   The works have been completed in accordance with the Contract, except due to minor outstanding work and defects, and
ii. A Taking-Over Certificate has been issued, or is deemed to have been issued in accordance with the Contract.

If the Contractor fails to pass the Tests on Completion, there are remedies available to the Employer. He may instruct further retesting until the Works pass, reject the Works if the failure deprives the Employer of substantially the whole benefit of the Contract, or issue a Taking-Over Certificate.

Prior to the commencement of the Tests on Completion, the Contractor shall submit to the Engineer the "as-built" documents and operation and maintenance manuals in accordance with the Specification and in sufficient detail for the Employer to operate, maintain, dismantle, reassemble, adjust and repair this part of the Works. Such part shall not be considered to be completed for the purposes of taking over until these documents and manuals have been submitted to the Engineer or Employer.

Due weightage may also be given to the value of outstanding work and the importance of defects to the safety of the facility. The Contract allows for minor outstanding works and defects to exist which do not substantially affect the intended purpose of the Works. In the FIDIC 1999 Red Book type of Contract, there is no obligation on the Contractor to ensure that the Works are fit for purpose, except where the Contractor takes on a design obligation. The Contractor's obligation is to construct the works as specified in the Contract. The Contractor applies for the Taking-Over Certificate by written notice. It is envisaged that the Contractor will anticipate completion and give notice up to a certain time, usually 14 days in advance of his expected completion date. It may be desirable for there to be a joint inspection of the Works or Section when the Contractor asserts that they are complete. This early notice allows the Employer time to take responsibility for the care of the Works. Once the Taking-Over Certificate is issued (or it is deemed to be issued) for the Works, a Section or a part, responsibility for its care passes from the Contractor to the Employer.

The Taking-Over Certificate also has significance in relation to the obligations to insure the Works, Plant, Materials, and Contractor's Documents. If the Employer issues a Taking-Over Certificate for a section of the Work, it may have the right to reclaim possession. However, if a Taking-Over Certificate is not issued for a part of the Work, the Employer is not allowed to use that specific portion of the Works, except in two cases: when the Employer uses the Works

a) As a temporary measure, as specified in the Contract, or

b) Agreed by both Parties.

What happens if the Employer does use any part of the Works? If the Employer uses a section of the Works before a Taking-Over Certificate is issued, then:

a) That part shall be deemed to have been taken over from the date it is used.

b) The Contractor ceases to be liable for the care of that part of the Works and

c) The Engineer (or Employer) shall issue a Taking-Over Certificate for that part if requested by the Contractor.

The failure to issue a Taking-Over Certificate, where a part of the Works is in commercial use or is permanently under the control of the Employer, could be a breach of contract on the part of the Employer. The Employer must also make sure that there is insurance in place in relation to damage to the Works and third parties. The Employer must also be aware that delay damages are reduced by a proportional amount to the value of the work Taken-Over.

If the Contractor suffers loss due to the Employer Taking-Over a part of the Works, it must give notice of its loss. The Contractor may claim Cost plus a reasonable profit. There may also be a mention of a right for the Contractor to an extension of time. If, in Taking-Over a part of the Works, the Employer impedes or delays the completion of a Section or the whole of the Works, then the Contractor may claim an extension of time. The Contract may state that the Contractor may claim an extension of the Time for Completion if it is delayed, impeded, or prevented by a cause attributable to the Employer, the Employer's Personnel, or the Employer's other contractors on the Site.

It should be noted that where the Employer Takes-Over a part of the Works, the Contractor may still be required to complete that part of the Works. In circumstances where the Employer is responsible for preventing the Tests on Completion from being carried out for more than a certain period, the Employer shall be deemed to have Taken Over the Works or Section.

The mere fact that the Employer prevents the Test on Completion from occurring for more than a certain period does not relieve the Contractor of his obligation to complete these tests. The Contractor must still carry out the Tests on Completion as soon as practicable and before the expiry of the Defects Notification Period. The Contractor may not have to give further notice that it is still ready to carry out the Test on Completion, but the Employer may have to give notice of the date when it wishes the tests to be carried out.

The Contract may include conditions for surfaces requiring reinstatement. Reinstatement has to be distinguished from repair and maintenance, particularly in circumstances where the Employer has moved onto and is making use of the surface concerned.

Section 11 – Defects Liability

As mentioned earlier, the defects liability period or the defects notification period is the time from when the employer starts using the facility up to a pre-defined period for observing defects in the constructed works.

The Contract usually requires that the Works shall be in the condition required by the Contract at the end of the Defects Notification Period. Where the Contractor carries out work in the Defects Notification Period, it is not entitled to receive payment if the work was a result of a defect in the design for which the Contractor was responsible.

Similarly, if the Plant, Materials, or workmanship are not in accordance with the Contract or there is a failure by the Contractor to comply with any other obligation, then the Contractor is required to remedy the problem without payment.

The Employer may obtain an extension of the Defects Notification Period if the Works, a Section, or a major piece of Plant cannot be used during the Defects Notification Period. The Contractor is required to remedy any defect during the Defect Notification Period, and if it does not, the Employer may claim against the Contractor. Rights are given to the Contractor to undertake this work subject to the Employer's reasonable security restrictions.

Once the Defects Notification Period has expired, the Employer is required, within a certain timeline, to issue a Performance Certificate. It is the Performance Certificate that is deemed to constitute acceptance of the Works. Under the FIDIC 1999 Red Book conditions, after the Performance Certificate has been issued, each Party will remain liable for the fulfillment of any obligation that remains unperformed at the time.

Where the Works are taken over in Sections, then it is possible for the Defects Notification Period to expire for one Section before another Section has been completed. Therefore, the Contract may refer to "the latest of the expiry dates of the Defects Notification Periods."

Completion of Outstanding Work and Remedying Defects. The obligation of the Contractor is to ensure that the Works and each Section shall be in a condition as required by the Contract at the end of the Defects Notification Period or as soon as practicable thereafter. The Contract usually:

a) Places a responsibility on the Contractor to complete all work which is outstanding at the date of the Taking-Over Certificate within such reasonable time as instructed by the Employer.
b) Requires the Contractor to execute all work required to remedy defects or damage, as may be notified by (or on behalf of) the

Employer on or before the expiry date of the Defects Notification Period.

The expression "Defects Notification Period" recognizes that the Contractor is obligated to remedy defects which are notified to it or instructed under this Sub-Clause.

However, not all damage or defects will be at the Contractor's risk and cost. For example, defects in the Employer's design will need to be remedied, but this will not be to the Contractor's account.

If the Employer does not permit the Contractor to rectify a defect, then any claim the Employer has will be limited to the cost it would have taken the Contractor to remedy the defects.

The failure to allow the Contractor to remedy the damage or defects would amount to a failure to mitigate a loss.

However, under the applicable law, the Employer may refuse to allow the Contractor to remedy defects if it has demonstrable grounds for believing that the Contractor would fail to carry out the work with the necessary skill and care.

After the Defects Notification Period has expired, the Employer may engage any third party to rectify defects instead of allowing the original Contractor to return.

The defects for which the Contractor could be responsible for are:

a) any design for which the Contractor is responsible,
b) Plant, Materials or workmanship not being in accordance with the Contract, or
c) Failure by the Contractor to comply with any other obligation.

The Defects Notification Period: cannot be extended by more than a certain period, usually two years. This is related to the dates for the Bonds and Guarantees issued by the Contractor.

Failure to Remedy Defects: The Contractor has a reasonable time to remedy any effect or damage. If the Contractor fails to remedy the defects within a reasonable time, then the Employer may fix a date when the works are to be carried out.

If there is a subsequent default by the Contractor, the Employer has the option to complete the work independently but at the Contractor's expense.

In cases where the Contractor cannot promptly rectify the defect or damage on the Site, it might be necessary to perform the remedial work on the Site. If the Contractor is not responsible for the defect and damage, it is entitled to payment as the work is carried out at the risk and cost of the Party liable. Suppose the Contractor considers that it is entitled to an additional payment for the Further Tests. In that case, it should promptly give notice and detailed particulars of its claim in accordance with the procedure specified in the Contract.

Right of Access: The Contractor is entitled to a right of access to the Works as may be required in order to remedy any defect or damage until the issue of the Performance Certificate. If there is a defect in the Works, the Employer may instruct the Contractor to search for the cause of it.

The Performance Certificate provides written confirmation that the Contractor has completed his obligations, and this document constitutes "acceptance of the Works." The Performance Certificate should be issued within specific timelines after the latest of the expiry dates of the Defects Notification Periods or as soon after that as the Contractor: (1) has supplied all the Contractor's Documents; (2) completed and tested all the Works; and/or (3) remedied any defects. It is clear that the Performance Certificate does not relieve the

Contractor of its liability for any defect discovered after the issue of that Certificate. The Performance Certificate is not final and conclusive, and the Contractor retains responsibility for the work it has carried out.

Contractors ought to be aware that their liability may continue until claims against them become time barred. Contractors ought also to be mindful that decennial liability may arise irrespective of the proper law of the contract as a mandatory rule of law of the place where the Works were constructed. Although a contractor may still have a liability after the Defects Notification Period and after the Performance Certificate is issued, that liability may usually be the one to pay damages and not necessarily to remedy defects. There could be exceptions for certain items like waterproofing, painting and any structural defects etc.

Both Employers and Contractors should take note that many forms of standard insurance, such as the Contractors' All Risk or Professional Indemnity Insurance, will not cover the Contractor after the works have been completed. The Works will, therefore, often be uninsured unless particular cover has been obtained.

Clearance of Site: The Contract may require the Contractor to remove its Equipment, materials, wreckage, rubbish, and Temporary Works. In the event that the Contractor fails to do this, the Employer may sell these items and will then account to the Contractor for the proceeds, minus any costs incurred. The Employer should ascertain whether the local law prohibits this action.

Section 12 – Measurement and Valuation

FIDIC 1999 is a re-measurement contract so that the Employer takes the risk of variations to the quantities and, in some instances, to the rates and prices that may be applied for the work executed. This may be different based on other standard or bespoke forms of

Contract.

If the Employer wishes to employ a Contractor on a lump-sum or cost-plus basis, then this clause needs to be deleted, or a different form of Contract may be used.

This condition deals with the measurement of the works. It usually does not include a reference to any standard method of measurement but states that the works are to be measured in accordance with the Bill of Quantities or other applicable Schedules. It may be a good idea to include a particular method of measurement, such as IS 1200 (in India), POMI, RICS NRM, SMM, CESSMM, or any such form of measurement as may be applicable. This condition deals with evaluating the appropriate rate or price for the works. There are three methods of evaluating the works: -

The rate or price specified for such item in the Contract; but if there is no such item, then:

a) The rate or price specified for similar work.
b) However, in certain specified circumstances, a new rate or price shall be appropriate.

It also deals with the valuation of omissions from the Work. As this is a re-measurement contract there is no assurance that the quantities measured in the Bill of Quantities are accurate. When quantities within the Bill of Quantities are exceeded, payment are usually processed at the rates set out in the Bill of Quantities.

In another section of the Contract, it is specified that the quantities, whether listed in the Bill of Quantities or any other Schedule, are considered estimated quantities and should not be regarded as precise and accurate quantities for the purpose of Measurement and Evaluation.

This condition is based upon the principle that the Works are to be valued by measuring the quantity of each item of work and then applying the appropriate rate per unit quantity or the appropriate lump-sum price.

If the Employer prefers to have a lump-sum contract, then this condition needs to be deleted or modified.

The Contract may also provide for a process that describes the procedure for measuring the quantity of each item of work. Quantities should preferably be agreed upon between the representatives of the Engineer and the Contractor as a continuing process and as the execution of the Works proceeds.

The contract may not specify any particular time in which measurements are to be taken.

Principles for measurement that is specified in a preamble to the Bill of Quantities,

- A publication which specifies principles of measurement and which is incorporated (by reference) into the Bill of Quantities, or
- For a contract which does not contain many or complex items of work, principles included in each of the item descriptions in the Bill of Quantities.

The FIDIC Guide states that "each item of the Works is to be measured in accordance with such principles/method of measurement, which takes precedence over any general.

A Bill of Quantities could be defined as: "A document that details the operations required to build any element of a standard construction project. It covers the input costs such as labor, materials, and plant, subcontracting, preliminaries, and overheads. It also covers the Contractor's profit or loss, the architect's and engineer's fees, and taxes as applicable.

A bill of quantities is structured to provide a weighted price for each component specified which, when summed across components, provide the purchasers' price for the standard construction project described." The Contractor must always take care to verify that the Bill of Quantities contains all item descriptions of work within the Drawings or Specification.

The Bill of Quantities comprises a detailed analysis of the design calculations, specifications, and drawings. The works are then divided into separate trades or types of activity, and a brief description of the activity is then provided. Quantities are then inserted – these quantities may be either estimated or calculated precisely. The rates within the Bill of Quantities are often a single rate compounded by the costs of labor and materials. The rates may or may not consider all the main costs incurred by a Contractor, such as temporary works. Bills of Quantities, therefore, may not reflect the real cost in the event that there are changes to the scope of the works.

The FIDIC Guide suggests that where there are omissions within the Bill of Quantities, which are discovered during the course of the works, then disputes may arise as to whether an additional item ought to be included. The FIDIC Guide suggests that this condition ought to be read as follows:

- If the Bill of Quantities includes (either incorporated by reference or specified) principles of measurement ***which clearly require that an item of work be measured***, and if the Bill of Quantities contains no such item, then an additional Bill item will be required in order to satisfy the requirement for measurement in accordance with such principles.
- If the Bill of Quantities includes (either incorporated by reference or specified) principles of measurement ***which do not clearly require that a particular item of work be measured***, and the work was as described in the Contract

and did not arise from a Variation, then measurement in accordance with such principles does not require the addition of a new Bill item.

- If the Bill of Quantities does not include principles of measurement for a particular item of work, and the work was as described in the Contract and ***did not arise from a Variation***, then measurement in accordance with such principles does not require the addition of a new Bill item.

The Employer and Contractor are required to agree or determine the value of each item of work, applying measured quantities to rates and prices in accordance with this condition. For each item, the appropriate rate or price shall be:

a) The rate or price specified for such item in the Contract; or
b) If there is no such item, the rate or price specified for similar works.
c) However, in certain defined circumstances, a new rate or price shall be specified.

The works as set out in the Specifications and Drawings are therefore valued in accordance with the rates and prices in the Contract. Additional quantities should also be valued in accordance with this ground where the work was specified in the Contract. The Contract could also specify whether a variation should be valued in accordance with this ground as the varied work is not work specified in the Contract. Point (b) above applies where there is no specified item for the work in the Contract, and therefore, a rate is used for similar work. The FIDIC Guide suggests that to establish "similarity of work," which pertains to work of a similar nature executed under comparable conditions, it is essential to consider both aspects. Although the works might be of a similar nature as outlined in the Contract, they may not necessarily be executed under similar conditions. (Perhaps there could be differences in the manner or the time when the works are carried out)

Numerous circumstances may arise where the Contractor may claim that works were not carried out under similar conditions. For example, there may be winter working rather than summer working, night rather than day working. Point (c) applies only in specific circumstances. It applies to mitigate the effects of points (a) and (b) if certain criteria are met. However, the Contract may specify criteria that are applicable wherein a new rate shall only be appropriate if all such criteria are satisfied. Therefore, it is possible for the Contractor to claim a new rate under the Contract on the basis of additional quantities. Some of the criteria are:

a) The measured quantity of the item of work must be less than 90%, or more than 110%, of the quantity stated in the Bill of Quantities. This criterion is consistent with the principle that Bill of Quantities provides only an estimate.

b) When the difference in quantity (namely, the difference between the Measured Quantity and quantity in the Bill of Quantities) is multiplied by the rate per unit quantity stated in the Bill of Quantities, the result must be more than 0.01% of the Accepted Contract Amount. This criterion is specified in order to avoid adjusting a rate if the adjustment will have little effect on the final Contract Price.

c) The difference in quantity (namely, the difference between the Measured Quantity and quantity in the Bill of Quantities) must have affected the "Cost per unit quantity", which is the Cost incurred executing the work covered by the item, divided by the quantity of the item as measurable in accordance with the applicable method of measurement.

d) The Contract must not have used phrase "fixed rate item" in relation to the item in the Bill.

If the four criteria are met, the Bill of quantity rate would typically be changed in proportion to such change in Cost per unit quantity which was the direct result of the change in quantity.

The Contract could specify criteria relating to work instructed under Variations. In these cases, a new rate or price will be considered appropriate if there is no Bill rate or price for work of similar character and executed under similar conditions. In other words, where there is a Variation, then evaluation under point (c) occurs only when the works, the subject of the variation, cannot be evaluated under points (a) or (b). If a new rate or price is to be assessed, it may be derived from relevant rates and/or prices in the Bill of Quantities or other appropriate Schedules and/or from reasonable Costs.

Further, it has to be noted that the Employer can omit work but cannot do so in order to have the work done by another Contractor. It is accepted that an Employer can omit work and have that work done by another contractor only if there are clear words in the contract. However, it may not be a fair condition, and the same has to be discussed and negotiated appropriately. A variation clause may entitle the employer to omit work that he no longer requires. This provision may entitle the Contractor to compensation for the costs reasonably incurred in the expectation of carrying out work subsequently forgotten. In some countries, the Employer may be allowed to omit a certain work and have it done by another contractor, but only after a cooling off period (usually one year or more).

Section 13 – Variations and Adjustments

This condition deals with the right of the Employer to vary the Contract. Usually, this right can be exercised at any time up to the issue of the Taking-Over Certificate. This condition could also deal with value engineering and permits the Contractor to propose a change that will benefit the Employer.

The proposal is prepared at the cost of the Contractor who designs the change. It deals with the procedure prior to the Employer instructing a variation. The Employer may request a proposal from the Contractor. However, while the Contractor is preparing the proposal, it must proceed with the works.

If the variation has to be paid in a different currency, the same can be specified in the Contract.

The Contract can also specify Provisional Sums, which could be defined as a sum (if any) which is specified in the Contract as a provisional sum for the execution of any part of the Works or for the supply of Plant, Materials, or services for which complete details may not be available at the time of entering into the Contract.

The Contract may also specify the inclusion of day work. This is where work of a minor or incidental nature is to be carried out. The work is then valued in accordance with the Day work Schedule in the Contract, or if there is no Day work Schedule, then the alternative method of payment as prescribed in the Contract. A day work schedule is a schedule that contains a pre-defined list of resources with pre-agreed unit rates per hour (or per day or per month) of utilization.

The Contract may also contain provisions to deal with costs arising from changes in the Laws of the Country which affect the Contractor in the performance of his obligations under the Contract.

Based on the commercial understanding between the Employer and the Contractor, the Contract may contain provisions that deal with adjustments for changes in cost. If this condition does apply, then the amounts payable to the Contractor for rises and falls in the cost of the Works are adjusted by a formula.

The Contractor shall execute and be bound by each Variation unless the Contractor promptly gives notice to the Engineer stating (with supporting particulars) that the Contractor cannot readily obtain the Goods required for the Variation. The Engineer shall cancel, confirm, or vary the instruction upon receiving this notice.

However, it should be noted that under the Contract, the Employer can omit quantities without limitation. Once again, and as discussed earlier, it is to be noted that an omission of quantities by the Employer cannot be instructed if the intention is to have the same work carried out by others.

This limitation may turn out to be very burdensome for some Employers. If, for some reason, a project has overrun its budget, the Employer may wish to omit part of the Work and only return when it has the money to do so.

If the Contract contains the above condition, it would prevent this strategy. However, if the Employer has realized during the course of the Works that the design or the working conditions have to be changed or has decided that it no longer needs the works, this provision may be used.

The Employer may instruct any additional work, Plant, Materials, or services necessary for the Permanent Works, including any associated Tests on Completion, boreholes, testing, and exploratory work. This provision is limited to additional work, etc, which is necessary for the completion of the Permanent Works as per the original scope of works. In other words, although this item refers to "additional work," it does not mean anything that changes the original concept of the Permanent Works.

The variation can also relate to changes to the sequence or timing of the execution of the Works. Like the earlier items listed above, this item does not allow for anything substantially different from the originally contemplated Works. The sequence or timing of the Works is normally under the control of the Contractor. The sequence and timing of the execution of the Works will have been set out in the Program provided by the Contractor, and the Contractor is required to proceed in accordance with the Program it submits.

The purpose of this provision may simply allow the Employer to require the Contractor to alter the elements of its program that relate to sequence and timing. Also, the change in timing does not refer to the speed at which the Contractor carries out his work but to the dates on which various events are to take place.

However, a change to timing could, in some circumstances, mean that the Work has to be carried out more quickly.

Thus, a Variation instruction under this condition could have the effect of requiring the Contractor to accelerate or slow down and, of course, to complete parts of the work at times it had not originally intended. However, this condition does not necessarily mean that the Employer can use his power of instructing a Variation to change the Time for Completion – only the sequence and timing of the Works in the interim.

The Contractor has the right to submit proposals for variations which may accelerate completion, reduce the cost either of completing the Works or of their ultimate maintenance or operation, improve the efficiency or the value of the Works, or otherwise benefit the Employer.

The proposal is provided at the Contractor's cost. It must include a description of the proposed changes and a program, details of any modifications necessary to the preexisting program, and the Time for Completion and the proposed payment. If the proposal requires a design change, then unless otherwise agreed upon, the new design will have to be prepared by the Contractor. If the change reduces the contract value, the Employer and the Contractor may agree to a fee payable by the Employer to the Contractor. The fee will usually be 50% of the benefit which the Employer derives from the variation.

The intention of this provision is to encourage Contractors to apply their knowledge and experience to benefit themselves and the Employer.

A Contractor may benefit in two ways from a variation it proposes. It may benefit because its costs of production are reduced, but the Employer receives a product that is as good as that designed initially. Alternatively, it may find a way to increase the value of the final product to the Employer without incurring additional costs.

If the Employer accepts a proposal that reduces the Contractor's cost of production without impacting the quality of the product received by the Employer, no adjustment is to be made to the contract sum. Similarly, if the proposal results in increased value to the Employer and either reduces or does not increase the Contractor's cost of production, no adjustment needs to be made. It is only where the reduced production cost is also matched by a reduction in final value or no change to the final value to the Employer that an adjustment has to be made. The Contract may provide for any incentives for schemes that increase the value to the Employer. An employer is likely to be pleased if its contractor develops an idea that increases the value of the Work without increasing the cost. Many Employers will be happy even if there is a lower increase in cost than the increased value. The only situation in which the Employer has a real incentive to accept such a proposal and pay a fee is where the Contractor proposes a method by which costs can be reduced without any reduction in the value of the final product.

Should a Contractor believe that it can produce a proposal that increases the value of the works at no cost or at a cost significantly less than the increase in value, it would need to persuade the Employer in advance to agree to a sharing of any benefits it can demonstrate. Similarly, if the proposal would produce an intangible benefit – such as early completion – there may be no clear mechanism built into the contract, and this would have to be agreed before the Contractor made an effort to produce a proposal.

A Provisional Sum may be included in the Contract because at the time the Contract is awarded, the Employer has not yet decided whether or not to instruct the Contractor to carry out the work which it covers. This may be because the relevant work is not already designed or because the Employer is not sure whether he wants, needs, or can afford it. It will be entirely at the discretion of the Employer whether the work is instructed, but the Contractor will be obliged to carry out the work if so instructed. An instruction to carry out work covered by a Provisional Sum is therefore not equivalent to a Variation. However, it may have a similar effect on the Contractor's progress and will obviously lead to additional payment. A provisional sum is usually included as a round-figure estimate. It is included mathematically in the original contract price, but the parties do not expect the initial round figure to be paid without adjustment. The contract usually provides expressly how it is to be dealt with. A typical clause in substance provides for the provisional sum to be omitted and an appropriate valuation of the work actually carried out to be substituted for it. A Contractor cannot program for works that are not foreseen. If the scope of the work increases, then this may entitle the Contractor to an extension of time. Furthermore, suppose the expenditure of the Provisional Sum arises because of an event that gives rise to an entitlement to an extension of time under the Contract, in that case, there should be no good reason why the Contractor would not be awarded an extension of time.

The Contract may contain a condition if a Day work Schedule is included in the Contract, which could be used for carrying out minor incidental works. In that case, a Variation can be instructed on the basis that it is paid for in accordance with the Schedule. Goods may not be ordered until the Contractor submits quotations to the Employer. The Contractor may need to submit proof of payment before being paid. The Contractor is required to deliver a daily breakdown in duplicate listing all items for which payment is due and including details of the personnel used, equipment and temporary Works used, and the quantities used. The Employer signs off on one copy. The Contractor then prices the resources and includes the cost in his next Interim Payment Certificate. Unlike the condition for Provisional sums, this is a true Variation provision. Its main effect is to provide an alternative method of valuation. The FIDIC Guide suggests that the Day work Schedule should contain the following:

a) A time charge rate for each person or category (money per person per hour, for example),
b) A time charge rate for each category of Contractor's Equipment (money per hour per item, for example), and
c) The payment due for each category of Materials.

However, for some Materials (for example, natural Materials and Materials manufactured on-site), it may be appropriate to provide items for pricing on a money-per-unit quantity basis. This condition specifically contemplates that someday, work items may not be the subject of separate payment. Thus, it is important that, if this is intended, the Day Works Schedule lists those items for which no payment is to be made.

In case the Contract provides, the Contract Price may need to be adjusted for increases or decreases in Cost resulting from changes to the law in the country where the works are being carried out. Changes to law include not only new laws or modifications to old laws but also changes of interpretation.

Adjustments will be made where the changes have taken place after the Base Date and where they affect the Contractor in the performance of the Contract. Where the Contractor is affected by a change in Law, he is required to give notice to the Engineer and may be entitled to an extension of time and/or Cost. In two respects, this provision has challenges:

a) Although the Contractor may be entitled to both an extension of time and to Cost, he will only be entitled to the extension of time if he cannot show that his Costs have increased.

b) The provision is limited to changes of law in the Country where the Works are being carried out. In an international project, the Contractor is as likely to be affected in another country as in the country where the Works are actually being taken place – much of the manufacture may be taking place off shore and materials and labor may well be being procured elsewhere.

There is thus an arbitrary distinction between changes in the Country of the Works and changes in other countries. Thus, it is recommended that this condition is discussed and negotiated in detail depending on the type and nature of the Contract.

Section 14 – Contract Price and Payment

This important clause sets out the method of payment, certificates, and release from liability.

The contract may contain conditions specifically dealing with advance payment guarantees. It could state that a guarantee has to be extended, and if the Contractor fails to do so, the Employer may invoke the bank guarantee to the extent that any part of the advance payment has not been repaid. The Advance Payment is to be made within a certain period of the Contractor providing his application together with the Performance Guarantee and Advance Payment Guarantee.

The contract may contain conditions related to applications for interim payment certificates. The Contractor is required to submit a Statement, which is then followed by the Interim Payment Certificate (IPC). There is usually a list of the items which have to be included in the Statement. These have been expanded to include Provisional Sums, any release of Retention Money, and the amount which the Employer is entitled to be paid for use of Temporary

Utilities. There could be a requirement that the Contractor is required to provide sufficient details along with the Statement. While this is obviously a useful and sensible requirement, it has significant implications. The Employer and the Contractor can have disagreements about what constitutes "sufficiency" or what the Employer needs to investigate regarding any claimed amounts.

Should there be such a disagreement and the Employer demands additional information, the time for payment under the Contract does not start to run until the relevant information has been received (there could, arguably, be a shortfall in the supporting documents, in case the same has not been agreed in the Contract).

Not only may the Contractor be paid later than it would otherwise be entitled, but it will also be limited in any claim for financing charges, if any, under the Contract. Unfortunately, it is sometimes possible for Employers to be slow in issuing IPCs, especially when the Employer is having payment difficulties. The Contractor would be very unwise not to comply with any demands for additional information, even if it considers the demands unreasonable. But even then, there may be a consequent delay in payment. It will be difficult for the Contractor to do anything which will speed up payment in these circumstances.

A Notice under the contract would be a drastic but possible remedy, but it could have the basis of a claim for Financing Charges at a later date.

However, it should be noted that the Contract may require the Employer to issue an IPC even in the absence of such information but make a suitable deduction to reflect his concerns. Hence, it is recommended to review, discuss, and negotiate the conditions relating to payments, as this would affect the cash flows of both the Contractor and the Employer.

Under the Contract, the Engineer /Employer was entitled to revise a payment schedule only if progress was less than expected. If the Schedule simply provides for fixed payments on a monthly basis, there will be the possibility of a dispute as to what progress was assumed in the Schedule of Payments.

The Contractor's principal obligation is to complete on time, not necessarily to conform to the program, and it is arguable that if it decides to change the way in which it will achieve timely completion, this does not mean that the agreed schedule of payments is inappropriate. In remeasured contracts, usually, the Contractor shall submit a periodic statement (usually once a month) showing the quantity of work done multiplied by the pre-agreed unit rate with adjustments of other elements as specified in the Contract.

Some contracts may allow the parties to agree that Plant and Materials may be paid for when shipped or delivered.

The Contractor simply provides the evidence in his application for payment, and the amount should then eventually be included in the IPC. It is thus probable that by the time the application is dealt with, the items will have been installed, causing further cash flow issues. The provision was intended to give the Contractor some early payment, but as amended, it may result in the opposite. Hence, it is recommended to negotiate this aspect, keeping in view the particular project requirements.

The Contractor is now entitled to a copy of each IPC, and it is specified that the Employer must explain any differences between the amount applied for and the amount Certified. Contractors will be very pleased to have an entitlement to this information.

It is further recommended from the point of view of Contractors that the Employer is now obliged to explain why amounts are withheld. Where Employer finds significant errors or discrepancies in the Statement, they now have a right to adjust the amount certified to take account of the extent to which this has prejudiced or prevented a proper investigation.

As before, the Employer's time for payment runs from when the Contractor makes the Application. This is usually 56 days for all IPCs except the Final Payment Certificate. The Final Payment Certificate is payable 56 days after its receipt by the Employer. Of course, these timelines may be negotiated by the Parties to suit the particular project.

Interest may be due on late payment.

The rate is usually calculated at a certain percentage above variously defined base rates that have been pre-defined.

The provision of the release of retention money has to be properly negotiated by the Parties as it would have a direct relation to the cash flow of both parties. Usually, the retention amount is held by the Employer till the Performance Certificate is issued (i.e., after the completion of the rectification of any defects). However, in some cases, a part of the retention amount is released by the Employer at an earlier date against the submission of a Retention bank guarantee by the Contractor. In certain other cases, the Employer may also agree to release a part of the retention amount after the Taking-over certificate has been issued. All of these options are acceptable and have to be discussed and negotiated at the time of signing the Contract.

Statement at Completion

This has always been required to include any amounts the Contractor considers to be due. The particular categories are now spelled out in detail – including claims still being considered by the Employer.

Final Statement

This is usually a statement prepared and submitted by the Contractor after the Performance Certificate has been issued. Negotiating the timelines by which certifications and payments would be made under the Contract is recommended.

Discharge

The Contract may provide for a full and final discharge by the Contractor, which may only take effect once all outstanding claims have been satisfied. This limitation may now pertain to the discharge covering all agreed amounts but with the ability to exclude only certain elements of the Contractor's claims.

The excluded items may only be items with respect to which a dispute or arbitration could be "in progress."

Thus, claims still being dealt with by the Employer cannot be excluded, nor can those which, while still living, have not yet been made the subject of a dispute or arbitration (notice not yet given, proceedings not yet commenced, etc.). Contractors' ought to be very reluctant to issue such a discharge, but it is a condition precedent to issue the Final Payment Certificate. The discharge will be deemed to have been submitted and will be effective even if the Contractor fails to provide it so long as the amount certified in the Final Payment Certificate has been paid and the Performance Security returned.

Issue of Final Payment Certificate

The Final Payment Certificate is usually issued 28 days after the Final Statement. The content of the statement now includes credit for any amounts paid under the Performance Security and any balance due from the Employer.

Cessation of Employer's Liability

The Employer's liability is limited by reference to what is included in the Final Statement unless something new arises after the work is completed.

Unless reference has been made in the Final Statement, the Employer is usually not liable for any amounts which the Contractor might wish to claim unless he makes a claim under the Contract within the prescribed timeline of receiving the Final Payment Certificate. Contractors will have to be sure to start all their claims immediately.

The cessation of the Employer's liability does not apply in the case of his indemnification obligations or in case of fraud, deliberate default, gross negligence or reckless misconduct.

Currencies of Payment

This condition deals with the way in which currencies are to be allocated in valuing variations. The other deals with the currencies in which Performance Damages are to be paid.

Section 15 – Termination by the Employer.

The contract may require the Employer to issue a Notice to the Contractor about a failure to carry out any obligation under the Contract. The Employer may demand that the Contractor rectify the failure and complete the remedy within a reasonable, specified time frame. Under the FIDIC 1999 Red Book, there are six grounds for termination by the Employer. These are as listed below:

i.   Failure of the Contractor to provide performance security or to comply with any notice to correct
ii. Contractor abandoning the work or demonstrating that he has no intention to continue the performance of his obligations under the Contract.
iii. Contractor failing to proceed in accordance with the agreed program

iv.   Contractor subcontracting or assigning the whole of the works without the express approval of the Employer

v.   Contractor becomes bankrupt or insolvent or goes into liquidation or any process which has a similar effect

vi.   The contractor offers a bribe, gift, inducement, reward, etc.

In most cases, the Employer may give 14 days' notice if it intends to terminate the Contract. However, if the Contractor has become bankrupt or insolvent or gives a bribe, gift, inducement, or reward, then the Employer may, by notice, terminate immediately. The Contractor must then leave the Site and deliver any required Goods, all Contractor's Documents, and other design documents made by or for him to the Employer.

Valuation at the date of Termination: When Termination has taken effect, the Employer is required to determine the value of the Works, Goods, and Contractor's Documents and any other sums due to the Contractor for Works executed in accordance with the Contract.

Payment after Termination: Once Termination has taken effect, the Employer may withhold further payments to the Contractor and recover from the Contractor any losses and damages incurred by the Employer and the extra costs of completing the Works.

Employer's Entitlement to Terminate: This is a termination at will or termination at convenience (of the Employer) provision that may allow the Employer to terminate the Contract by giving notice, so long as the Employer does not intend to have the Works executed by himself or another contractor.

Section 16 –Suspension and Termination by the Contractor.

The Contractor may have a right to suspend work in the event that the Employer fails to certify in accordance with conditions relating to Payment Certificates or the Employer fails to comply with conditions relating to Employer's Financial Arrangements or Payment.

Prior to the Contractor suspending work, it may need to give a certain notice period. The right to suspend may not affect the Contractor's entitlement to terminate or claim financing charges. In the event that the Contractor suffers delay or cost as a result of suspension, it may need to give an appropriate notice.

Termination by the Contractor. There are usually seven grounds specified in the Contract due to which the Contractor may terminate the Contract.

These conditions are as listed below:

i.   The Employer failing to provide evidence of Employer's financial arrangements, if requested for by the Contractor and if provided for in the Contract.

ii.   The Employer failing to issue the payments certificate within the timelines agreed in the Contract

iii.   The Employer failing to make the payments within the timelines agreed in the Contract

iv.   The Employer failing to perform his other obligations under the contract

v.   The Employer failing to execute a Contract agreement or assigning the contract without the consent of the Contractor

vi.   The Employer suspends the works for a prolonged period of time which affects the whole of the works.

vii.   The Employer becoming bankrupt, insolvent or goes into liquidation or any event that has a similar effect.

In most cases, the Contractor may give notice if it intends to terminate the contract. However, if there has been a prolonged suspension or bankruptcy, liquidation, or insolvency, the Contractor may terminate immediately by notice.

Cessation of Work by the Contractor and Removal of the Contractor's Equipment.

This provision applies in all those circumstances where the termination is not the result of the Contractor's fault.

Upon termination under the specific conditions, the Contractor shall promptly:

a) Cease all further work, except for such work as may have been instructed by the Employer for the protection of life or property or for the safety of the Works,

b) Hand over Contractor's Documents, Plant, Materials and other work, for which the Contractor has received payment, and

c) Remove all other Goods from the Site, except as necessary for safety, and leave the Site.

Under the Contract, the Contractor may be required to hand over the Contractor's Documents, Plant, Materials, and other work for which the Contractor has received payment. The term "Contractor's Documents" may include documents of a technical nature (including computer programs, software, drawings, designs and models) supplied by the Contractor under the Contract. The cost of these is unlikely to be separately mentioned in the payment provisions of the Contract – if the contract has Bills of Quantity, payment for them may be included in the Preliminaries, in which case it may still be hard to tell whether they are paid for. More likely, there will be a provision that the cost of such items is included in the rates or prices for physical items of work. The Contractor will probably expect to recover the cost of these items over the term of the contract within the rates or prices for other items. Thus, where there is a premature end to the Contract, it could be arguable whether they have been paid for. There should be no such problem with Plant and Materials, which are defined as items that are to be incorporated into the Permanent Works.

Payment on Termination

If the Contractor terminates under respective provisions of the Contract, the Employer may be required to promptly:

a) Return the Performance Security to the Contractor,
b) Pay the Contractor in accordance with provisions of the Contract, and
c) Pay to the Contractor the amount of any loss of profit or other loss or damage sustained by the Contractor as a result of this termination. (if the same is clearly agreed within the contract)

Section 17 – Risks and Indemnity

The conditions pertaining to Risk and Responsibility may also set out other provisions relating to indemnities, limitation of liability, and the specific topic of intellectual and industrial property rights. This condition provides that the Contractor assumes responsibility and bears the risk for the care of the works during execution and for remedying any defects during the Defects Notification Period. The transfer of risk to the Employer occurs upon the issuance of the Taking-Over Certificate for the portion of the works that are defined as completed. Generally, in construction contracts, 'risk' is understood to mean an event or circumstance that causes delay, loss, or damage to the Works. A risk can be attributed to either the Employer or the Contractor or remain neutral in terms of its origin. The purpose of risk allocation is to determine which party bears the risk for such events. The Contractor may be required to remediate the damage at his own cost, or the Employer may be required to pay for the damaged works.

In respect of indemnities, the insurance provisions of the Contract relate to risks and indemnities and should be considered together to ascertain the scope of indemnities for losses that are not covered by insurance (or otherwise non-recoverable). Where the contract fails to set out who bears the risk of loss, then the substantive law of the contract must be considered.

Under the contract, the responsibility of the risk for certain types of claims is allocated by way of indemnities so that each party indemnifies the other for the consequence of such a claim.

a) Personal injury
b) Damage to personal or real property (other than the Works)
c) Other specific matters for which the Employer indemnifies the Contractor

The Contractor is required to give a wide indemnity against "all claims, damages, losses, and expenses" in respect of these types of damage. The indemnity would include legal fees. The indemnity is not subject to any exclusion of liability for loss of profit, loss of contract, or other indirect losses. The Contractor is obliged to indemnify not only the Employer but also the 'Employer's Personnel and respective agents.' This covers any personnel who have been 'notified' to the Contractor by the Employer and assistants delegated with authority. Visitors on site or any specialist advisors must be notified to the Contractor to ensure that the indemnity covers such persons.

Similarly, the Employer has the equivalent obligation to indemnify the Contractor and the 'Contractor's Personnel and their respective agents' with respect to claims, damages, losses, and expenses for death and personal injury and specific matters that may be excluded from insurance coverage. This captures any personnel 'assisting' with the work. However, the difference here is that there is no requirement to notify the Employer of such persons. The Employer indemnity will, therefore, capture those falling within the category.

Each party is obligated to provide indemnification and protect the other party from any claims or liabilities.

The Indemnity Provisions Relate To:

Personal Injury- Both Contractor and Employer are responsible for claims relating to personal injury (bodily injury, sickness, disease, or death). The indemnity obligation applies to personal injury caused to any persons, which may include each Party's personnel. The insurance obtained in compliance with the contract terms will offer coverage for losses in cases of personal injury to individuals other than the Contractor's personnel, as well as cases of personal injury to the Contractor's personnel. For losses not recoverable under a particular policy, the Contractor bears the risk by way of its indemnifying obligation for personal injury claims which may arise "out of or in the course of or by reason of the Contractor's design (if any), execution and completion of the Works and the remedying of any defects."

The Contractor remains responsible for the acts or defaults of any of its Subcontractor(s) or its agents and employees.

The Contractor's responsibility runs from the Commencement Date (and the execution of the Works commences as soon as is reasonably practicable after that) and ends on the issue or deemed issue of the Taking-Over Certificate for the Works, Section, or part of the Works (or up to the completion of the Defects Notification Period, if the Contract specifies).

The Taking-Over Certificate may record that the Works or Section was completed on an earlier date than the issue date of the Certificate. Given that liability does not pass to the Employer until the issue date (or deemed issue date), the Contractor may, in certain circumstances, remain responsible for the Works for the gap between the actual taking over date and the date of issue of the relevant Taking-Over Certificate or deemed issue. For insurance purposes, it is usually the issue of the Taking-Over Certificate and not the date stated in the certificate, which is relevant.

Employer's Risks must be considered in conjunction with conditions relating to risks and indemnities. The FIDIC Guide mentions that Employer Risks may constitute a force majeure event depending on the severity and adverse consequence of the risk event.

If war occurs and the Contractor is prevented from carrying out the Works (but there is no damage to the Works), the Contract may not assist the Contractor. In order to recover time and cost, the Contractor will have to rely on force majeure conditions.

Risks may cause the Contractor delay or result in additional costs for the Contractor. The Employer may bear the risk for rectifying loss and damage that occurred to the Works, Goods, or Contractor Documents as a result of the risks.

Intellectual and Industrial Property Rights: This condition deals with the Employer's and Contractor's respective responsibilities for "claims" arising out of "infringement" of intellectual property rights relating to the Works and the indemnity obligations for each Party against certain claims.

Under this condition, the term 'other Party' is usually (not always) used to describe the Party who is entitled to an indemnity under this condition. There are separate indemnities for the Employer and the Contractor for claims made against a Party by a third-party alleging infringement of their rights.

There is usually a defined list of specific matters constituting an infringement or an alleged infringement as set out below:

• Patent
• Registered design

- Copyright
- Trade mark
- Trade name
- Trade secret
- Other intellectual property right or other industrial property right 'relating to the Works'.

The Employer's improper use is either:

a) For a purpose not provided in the Contract or reasonably inferred from the contract, or
b) In conjunction with anything not supplied by the Contractor (unless such use was disclosed to the Contractor in the Contract or prior to the Base Date).

The Contractor has a limited indemnity obligation to the Employer. The Contractor is required to indemnify the Employer for claims 'arising out of or in relation to':

1. The manufacture, use, sale, or import of any 'Goods'. 'Goods' means the Contractor Equipment, Materials, Plant, and Temporary Works used for execution and completion of the Works to include the remedy of defects.

2. Any design for which the Contractor is responsible.

The Parties must co-operate where claims arise for items which are being contested by the indemnifying Party.

The indemnifying party may conduct negotiations to settle the claim or deal with litigation or arbitration that may arise and against which it is liable to indemnify the other Party.

The other Party, including its Personnel, must assist in contesting the claim. The indemnifying Party is liable for the costs incurred by the other Party in assisting it in contesting the claim. The other Party (and its Personnel) may be in breach of Contract if they make any admission which might be 'prejudicial' to the indemnifying Party without the consent of the indemnifying Party. The exception to this is where the other Party requests the indemnifying Party to take over the conduct of any negotiations, litigation, or arbitration, but the indemnifying Party fails to do so.

A Party receiving the claim must give notice to the other Party within a certain period from the date of receipt of that claim. A Party failing to give notice of the claim may be deemed to have waived 'any' right to an indemnity under the Contract.

The purpose of the sanction is to provide a strong incentive for the indemnifying Party to inform the other Party in good time so as to enhance the opportunity for the other Party to defend and assist in contesting the claim.

Usually, there is no time limit on the indemnity obligations.

Limitation of Liability

As with most other forms of contract nowadays, one of the purposes of the introduction of this sub-clause is to assist the parties in appraising their risks at the contract negotiation stage. On a practical level, it is presumably intended to enable the parties to identify and insure (so far as they can) their potential liabilities under the Contract.

This condition may state that neither Party shall be liable to the other for certain types of loss, i.e., loss of use of any Works, loss of profit, loss of any contract, or for any indirect or consequential loss or damage which may be suffered by the other Party in connection with the Contract. These clauses will generally be upheld. It should be noted that loss of Works, loss of profit, and loss of Contract may include both direct and consequential losses.

The Contract may go on to limit the Contractor's liability to the Employer under or in connection with the Contract (except in certain situations) to the sum inserted in the Particular Conditions or, if that sum is not stated, a certain percentage of the Accepted Contract Amount. There may be no similar restriction on the Employer's liability to the Contractor.

Lastly, in the event of fraud, deliberate default, or reckless misconduct by the party in default, this condition may not apply to limit its liability.

Section 18 – Insurances

The insurances under the contract have to be discussed and negotiated in detail at the contract negotiation stage. Insurances may include but may not be limited to the following:

i. Contractor's All risk insurance
ii. Workmen Compensation policy
iii. Third Party Insurances
iv. Marine insurance
v. Plant and machinery insurance
vi. Professional Indemnity insurance

Section 19 – FORCE MAJEURE

This condition has already been covered in Chapter 2. Hence the only purpose on bringing this for discussion at this point is to ensure that it is listed out, discussed, and negotiated appropriately during contract negotiations.

Section 20 – Disputes

The whole purpose of this book is to educate the readers to negotiate all contracts in a guided manner so that disputes are avoided. Hence, the aspect of disputes has been kept out of the context of this book. However, a few points to keep in mind while negotiating the dispute related clauses are below:

i. The first attempt must always be towards an amicable settlement between the Employer and the Contractor without involving any third party

ii. The next attempt could be towards alternate dispute resolution methods such as Mediation or Arbitration. In this regard, it would also be a good idea to define the number of arbitrators that the Parties wish to appoint. It is usually in odd numbers such as one, three, five, etc.

iii. Formal litigation in courts should always be the last resort

iv. The venue and seat of arbitration have to be thought through at the initial stage as this could add to the costs of the parties in the event of a dispute

Call to Action:

The above is a set of conditions that would be applicable to any type of contract. I would like to call the reader to examine the contracts that you are currently working on and explore how the above conditions are addressed within your contracts. You can share your thoughts on www.prasamviidah.com or write to manish.mohandas@outlook.com

CHAPTER 5:

KNOW YOUR CLIENT OR VENDOR

So far, we have understood the entire process of bidding or tendering for a project. We have covered getting into a contract agreement and the types of standard forms of contract available for use. Following that, we discussed the significant terms and conditions.

This was followed by a detailed discussion on other terms and conditions using the FIDIC 1999 standard form of contract. It is now time to understand the person or organization with whom we will enter into this contract agreement. We should understand the person or the organization before we commence discussions on the project.

However, it is best to understand this at least before getting into an agreement. This is important due to the complex business world we are all in today. If we get into a deal with a person or an organization whose capabilities have not been fully understood, we are at a high risk of failure.

On the other hand, even if we enter into an agreement with a person or an organization with full awareness of their weaknesses, we can plan to supplement the shortcomings to ensure that the works are not affected.

Hence, this aspect is essential. While the technical and commercial capabilities would have been assessed, it is best to know the person or an organization from a legal framework.

Individual Persons

For smaller projects where the contract agreement is between two individuals, the risk may be low. However, it is recommended to understand the person from various aspects such as:

1. History of successful projects delivered
2. Competence and capability of the person (or their support team, if applicable)
3. Payments history (for the Client) and payments history of suppliers (for the Contractor)
4. Ease of doing business with person. i.e. is the person litigative or collaborative.

Organizations

While dealing with organizations, it is important to consider at least the following aspects:

1. Types of legal entities
2. Authorized signatories/Board resolution
3. Ease of doing business
4. Assessing company performance
5. Supplier payments etc.

Types of Legal Entities

Multiple types of organizations in India provide various opportunities and risks from a business perspective. For example, the types of organizations in India are One-person companies (OPC), partnership companies, limited liability partnerships (LLP), private limited companies, and limited companies. In addition to these, there are other forms of companies, such as Section 8 companies, Trusts, and Society. Each of these types of organizations has multiple advantages and also poses risks. While conducting international business, it is also essential to understand the types of companies in the respective countries. It is best to consult a professional chartered accountant and/or a lawyer to obtain detailed advice on the risks associated with a particular type of company in relation to a new contract to be executed. The details of organizations that are registered with the Ministry of Corporate Affairs, India, are available on www.mca.gov.in

Let us have a closer look at the various types of legal entities (organizations or companies) in India.

Public Limited Company in India

A Public Limited Company is one of the first types of business entities in India that is commonly used for large-scale operations, such as infrastructure projects or manufacturing. Public limited companies are required to have a minimum of three directors and a minimum of seven shareholders, but they can have an unlimited number of shareholders. One of the key advantages of a Public Limited Company is that it can raise large amounts of capital by issuing shares to the public. These shares can be traded freely on a stock exchange once the company is listed, which can help to increase liquidity. Additionally, since a Public Limited Company is a separate legal entity, the personal assets of the shareholders are protected in case of bankruptcy or insolvency.

However, incorporating a Public Limited Company in India can be a complex and time-consuming process. It requires compliance with various legal and regulatory requirements, such as obtaining a certificate of incorporation, filing multiple forms with the Registrar of Companies, and obtaining necessary approvals from the Ministry of Corporate Affairs. Public Limited Companies are also subject to more stringent regulations and reporting requirements than other business entities in India. For example, they are required to hold regular board meetings and annual general meetings, prepare and file audited financial statements, and disclose certain information to the public.

Despite these challenges, a Public Limited Company can benefit entrepreneurs and investors in India significantly. Providing access to a large pool of investors can help to raise capital quickly and efficiently, which is critical for companies seeking to expand or pursue new opportunities. Additionally, the legal protections offered to shareholders can reduce risk and increase investors' confidence. Overall, a Public Limited Company is a powerful tool for businesses seeking to grow.

Private Limited Company in India

A Private Limited Company is a common choice for small and medium-sized businesses in India, representing one of the various types of business entities. It is a privately held entity and is considered an independent legal entity once incorporated. Private limited companies have a minimum of one and a maximum of fifty shareholders, and they can have a minimum of two and a maximum of fifteen directors. Unlike Public Limited Companies, Private Limited Companies cannot publicly trade their shares. The shares are typically held by a small group of investors, such as family members or close associates.

One of the key advantages of a Private Limited Company is that it provides a flexible and scalable structure for businesses to grow and expand. The company's legal structure allows for a separate legal identity, meaning it can enter into contracts, own assets, and sue or be sued in its own name. This structure provides greater legal protection to the shareholders, who are not personally liable for the debts or obligations of the company.

Another advantage of a Private Limited Company is that it allows for greater control over the business. Unlike publicly traded companies, Private Limited Companies are not subject to the scrutiny of outside investors or the public. This means that the owners and directors have greater freedom to make decisions that are in the best interests of the company and its stakeholders.

However, there are also some disadvantages to a Private Limited Company in India. For example, the process of incorporating a Private Limited Company can be time-consuming and requires compliance with various legal and regulatory requirements. Additionally, the shares of the company cannot be publicly traded, which can make it more challenging to raise capital compared to a Public Limited Company. Finally, the company's operations are subject to greater scrutiny from regulatory authorities, which can increase compliance costs and administrative burdens.

Joint-Venture Company in India

One of the business entities in India is a Joint Venture (JV). In a JV, the partners jointly share the profits, losses, management responsibilities, and operational expenses of the new business entity. This arrangement allows foreign companies to tap into the well-established contact network, distribution channels, and marketing resources of their Indian partners, which can help them establish a foothold in the Indian market. One of the key advantages of a JV is that it allows foreign investors to leverage the expertise and knowledge of their Indian partners. For example, an Indian partner may deeply understand local market conditions, consumer preferences, and regulatory requirements that can be invaluable to a foreign company looking to enter the Indian market. The JV structure also enables the investors to jointly manage the risks involved with the new business and limit their individual exposure by sharing the liabilities. Another advantage of a JV is that it can provide access to financial resources that may be difficult to obtain on an individual basis. For example, the Indian partner may have access to government grants, subsidies, or other forms of financial assistance that can help to fund the new business entity.

Additionally, the partners can pool their resources to finance the startup costs of the business, such as research and development expenses, marketing and advertising costs, and other operational expenses. However, there are also some disadvantages to consider when establishing a JV as one of the types of business entities in India. For example, the partners may have different expectations, cultures, and business practices that can create friction and conflict. Also, the legal and regulatory requirements for setting up a JV can be complex and time-consuming, which can add to the overall cost of establishing the new business entity. Furthermore, the partners may have different ideas about managing the business, which can lead to disagreements and conflicts.

Partnership Firm in India

A Partnership Firm in India is a type of business entity where two or more individuals come together and share profits and losses in a mutually agreed ratio. As per the Indian Partnership Act, of 1932, the owners of a partnership firm are individually known as partners and collectively known as a firm. To start a partnership business in India, a minimum of two people is required, and the maximum number of partners is ten. The partners have unlimited liability, which means they are personally liable for the debts and obligations of the partnership firm. One of the main advantages of a partnership firm is its flexibility and ease of formation. It is relatively simple to form and does not require any mandatory registration.

Additionally, a partnership firm can utilize each partner's skills, expertise, and resources to run the business effectively. However, a partnership firm is not a separate legal entity; thus, its existence depends on the partners. This means that a partner's death, retirement, or insolvency can lead to the dissolution of the firm. Also, since each partner has unlimited liability, entering into a partnership agreement with someone with a poor financial track record can be risky. Therefore, it is essential to have an explicit partnership agreement that outlines the roles, responsibilities, profit-sharing ratio, and exit strategies of the partners.

One Person Company in India

One Person Company is a relatively new type of company in India, which was introduced in 2013 as part of the Companies Act. As the name suggests, this type of business entity can be owned and managed by a single person. However, only Indian residents are eligible to incorporate an OPC, and foreigners are not permitted to do so. The key benefit of a One Person Company is that it provides a unique opportunity for individual entrepreneurs to start their own businesses without having to involve other shareholders or partners. As a result, it enables entrepreneurs to have complete control over the decision-making process and offers a simplified and streamlined process for running a business.

Moreover, One Person Company enjoys the benefits of a private limited company, such as limited liability protection, separate legal entity status, and perpetual succession. The liability of the owner is limited to the extent of their investment in the company, which means that the personal assets of the owner are protected from any financial obligations or debts incurred by the company. However, there are also some disadvantages to consider. One of the main limitations of One Person Company is that it can only have one director, which may limit the scope of the business. Additionally, since One Person Company is a relatively new concept in India, it may not enjoy the same level of credibility and trust as more established business entities such as private limited companies. Finally, like any other company, One Person Company is required to comply with various legal and regulatory requirements, which may be time-consuming and costly for small businesses.

Sole Proprietorship in India

A sole proprietorship in India is a form of business entity where a single individual handles the entire business organization. This type of business structure is ideal for those who want to run a small, localized business with limited resources and capital investment. The owner of a sole proprietorship is the sole recipient of all profits but is also personally liable for all losses incurred by the business.

This type of company is best suited for limited and localized markets, where customers give importance to personal attention. One of the main advantages of a sole proprietorship is that there are fewer legal formalities, as a proprietorship does not have a separate legal existence. This makes it easier and quicker to set up and operate compared to other types of business entities in India. However, because the owner is personally responsible for all the liabilities and debts incurred by the business, there is a significant amount of risk involved. Another disadvantage of a sole proprietorship is that it can be challenging to raise capital or expand the business beyond a certain point. Since the company is solely owned and operated by one person, securing additional funding or attracting investors may be difficult.

Moreover, if the owner passes away or cannot run the business due to health reasons, the business may come to a halt unless a successor can take over. Despite these drawbacks, sole proprietorship remains a popular choice for small business owners in India, particularly those in the service industry, such as freelancers, consultants, and small retail shops.

Branch Office in India

A branch office is an extension of a foreign company engaged in manufacturing and trading activities outside India. It is not allowed to undertake manufacturing activities on its own but can subcontract those to an Indian manufacturer. The primary objective of a branch office is to represent the parent company in India and conduct activities related to its business. Before starting operations, the branch office must obtain approval from the Reserve Bank of India (RBI). Branch offices are not allowed to undertake commercial activities of any nature, and all income generated must be remitted back to the parent company. The advantages of setting up a branch office in India include access to a large market, lower establishment costs, and a better understanding of local regulations. However, disadvantages include:

i. Limited decision-making autonomy.
ii. Lack of complete control.
iii. Potential issues related to cultural differences and communication.

Non-Government Organization

Non-Government Organizations or Non-profit Companies are citizen-based associations that operate independently of the government, usually to serve a social purpose. Non-Governmental Organizations are not intended to gain profits. They work towards promoting a cause or development project for the betterment of society.

They can be set up as Trusts, Societies, or Section 8 Companies. Non-Government Organizations in India often work towards alleviating poverty and promoting education, healthcare, environmental conservation, and other social issues. These organizations rely on donations, grants, and funding from individuals, government agencies, and international organizations to carry out their operations. The main advantage of Non-Governmental Organizations is that they allow individuals to contribute towards a social cause, making a difference in society. However, the disadvantage is that setting up Non-Government Organizations can be a long and complicated process due to the regulatory and legal formalities involved in the registration process.

Apart from examining the legal entities in India, let's explore the different legal structures in some of the countries worldwide. (Source: Reference number 28)

ARGENTINA

Corporation (Sociedad Anónima or SA) - This is a separate and distinct legal entity. Admits a minimum of 2 shareholders. It is managed by a board of directors, who are elected by the stockholders of the corporation.

Single-Shareholder Corporation (Sociedad Anónima Unipersonal or SAU) - This is a separate and distinct legal entity. Admits exclusively one shareholder. It is managed by a board of directors who are elected by the corporation's only stockholders.

Simplified Corporation (Sociedad por Acciones Simplificada or SAS) - This is a separate and distinct legal entity. Admits one or more shareholders. It is managed by a board of directors who are elected by the stockholders. Its incorporation and development are entirely digital.

Limited Liability Company (Sociedad de Responsabilidad Limitada or SRL) - This is a separate and distinct legal entity. Admits a minimum of 2 members and a maximum of fifty. They are managed by a single manager or several managers with full powers who may act individually or by a Board of Managers acting by majority, appointed by the members.

AUSTRALIA

Branch - It is possible for foreign companies to conduct business in Australia through a branch office. A foreign company may establish a branch in Australia by registering with the Australian Securities and Investments Commission (ASIC) as a foreign company carrying on business in Australia. It must also appoint a local agent who will be responsible for ensuring the foreign company's compliance with the Corporations Act 2001 (Cth).

Proprietary company - A proprietary company is a limited liability company designed for 50 shareholders or fewer. It is the most common type of company in Australia, and it has the advantage of being more straightforward and less expensive to administer than a public company. It is managed by a board of directors, which is responsible for making business decisions and overseeing the general affairs of the company. Directors may be appointed by other directors or shareholders and removed by an ordinary resolution of the shareholders.

Public Company - Similar in concept to a proprietary company, but there is no limit on the number of shareholders. There is also no limit on the ability of a public company to raise funds from the public, subject to satisfying applicable disclosure requirements.

AUSTRIA

General Partnership (Offene Gesellschaft, OG) - This entity, involved in trading activities, holds its partners fully responsible for their debts, risking their entire assets. At the same time, all partners are managers of the business. Individuals or entities who are not partners must not be involved in the partnership's management.

Limited Partnership (Kommanditgesellschaft, KG) - This entity engages in trading activities. It is comprised of one or more general partners, and these individuals assume unlimited joint and several liability for all the debts of the partnership. Additionally, there are one or more limited partners within this entity. These limited partners choose to restrict their liability for the entity's debts to a specific amount, which they commit to paying to the entity. Those whose liability is restricted are excluded from the management of the limited partnership. External managers must not be appointed.

Limited Liability Company (Gesellschaft mit beschränkter Haftung, GmbH) - Separate and distinct legal entity. They are managed by their managers (may be shareholders or external individuals), who are responsible for making business decisions and the operations of the company. Managers may be elected by the shareholders of the company or may be appointed in the articles of association. Managers may be shareholders of the company.

Stock Corporation (Aktiengesellschaft, AG) - Separate and distinct legal entity. They are managed by their management board (comprising at least one individual), which is responsible for making major business decisions and overseeing the general affairs of a corporation. The supervisory board of a corporation elects the management board. The supervisory board (mandatory for stock corporations) must be comprised of at least three individuals, and the management board must supervise it.

BAHRAIN

If entities wish to conduct business in Bahrain, they must establish a presence in the country.

The most commonly adopted legal structures in Bahrain are limited liability companies (WLL), closed shareholding companies (BSC(c)), and foreign branches (branches).

With Limited Liability (WLL) - A WLL in Bahrain is a private company with one or more shareholders; each of them shall only be liable to the extent of their respective shareholding in the company.

A WLL can be owned by a single natural or legal person. WLLs can neither engage in banking and insurance activities nor can they issue any shares, negotiable warrants, or debentures to the public.

Closed Shareholding Company (BSC(c)) - A BSC(c) is a company that consists of at least two shareholders who underwrite negotiable shares among themselves without underwriting such shares to the public. The shares of a BSC(c) cannot be offered to the public. Unlike a WLL, a BSC(c) is allowed to carry out banking and insurance activities.

Foreign Branch (Branch) - A foreign company that is incorporated abroad may establish a branch office in Bahrain if it provides a guarantee letter from the parent company to take full responsibility for the branch.

BELGIUM

Public Limited Company (*société anonyme/naamloze vennootschap*) – This is a separate and distinct legal entity. Two types of board structures may be chosen (i.e., monistic board structure or dualistic board structure). If the monistic board structure is selected, the public limited company may be managed by either a collegial board of at least three directors or two directors in case there are less than three shareholders or, if provided by the articles of association, a sole director. The collegial board is responsible for making major business decisions and overseeing the general affairs of the company. Managing directors (or general managers), who run the company's day-to-day operations, are appointed by the directors.

The dualistic board structure must be provided for in the articles of association and consists of a board of supervision and an executive board. The board of supervision is a collegial board of at least three members and is elected by the shareholders of the company. Members of the board of supervision cannot simultaneously be members of the executive board. The board of supervision is responsible for the general policy and strategy of the public limited company and has reserved competencies. The executive board is a collegial board of at least three members. The members of the board of supervision appoint members of the executive board. The executive board has complete management competence except for the ones reserved by the law for the shareholders' meeting and those reserved for the board of supervision.

Limited Company (société à responsabilité limitée/besloten vennootschap) – This is a separate and distinct legal entity. It is managed by either a sole director, a non-collegial board of directors, or a collegial board of directors (if provided in the articles of association), who are responsible for making major business decisions and overseeing the general affairs of the limited company. Directors are elected by the shareholders of the limited company. The management body may appoint one or more persons who can act alone, jointly, or collegially and who are responsible for the daily management. If the management body appoints no team for daily management, the day-to-day operations of the company are run by the director(s), who has/have, in principle, full authority.

Belgian Branch Office of a Foreign Company - No separate and distinct legal entity from the foreign company. The legal representative must represent the foreign company with regard to the activities of its Belgian branch office.

BRAZIL

Limited Liability Company (Sociedade Limitada) - Sociedades Limitadas are regulated by Law 10,406/02 (Brazilian Civil Code) and residually, whenever set forth in their articles of organization, by Law 6,404/76, as amended, which regulates Brazilian corporations. A Sociedade Limitada is simple to incorporate and operate as very few formalities are required for its organization and management. The Sociedade Limitada is managed by the officers/managers, who run the corporation's day-to-day operations and may also have a board of directors, who, if appointed, will be responsible for making major business decisions and overseeing the company's general affairs. The officers must be individuals appointed either by the board of directors or by the quota holders' meeting, especially when the company lacks a board of directors. Meanwhile, the directors are elected by the company's quota holders. The management structure of a Sociedade Limitada is established in the company's articles of association.

Corporation (Sociedade Anônima) - Legal entity suitable for several types of businesses and investments. Non-listed corporations are simple to incorporate and operate, but more formalities are required for their organization and management when compared to the Sociedade Limitada. One example is the mandatory publication of certain corporate acts. The Sociedade Anônima is managed by the officers, who run the day-to-day operations of the corporation, and, in some instances, by a board of directors, which is responsible for making major business decisions and overseeing the general affairs of the corporation. The officers must be individuals appointed by the board of directors or by the shareholders' meeting, in case the corporation does not have a board of directors, whilst the directors are elected by the corporation's shareholders. The management structure of a Sociedade Anônima is established in the corporation's bylaws, and certain corporations, such as publicly held corporations, shall mandatorily appoint a board of directors.

CANADA

Corporate Subsidiary (corporation form rather than flow-through form) – This is a separate and distinct legal entity. May incorporate federally (under the Canada Business Corporations Act) or provincially/territorially – for example, under the Business Corporations Act (Ontario). It is managed by a board of directors, which is responsible for making major business decisions and overseeing the general affairs of the corporation. Directors are elected by the shareholders of the corporation. Officers who run the day-to-day operations of the corporation are appointed by the directors. Additional forms of entity structures also exist and could be helpful in some instances but are not covered in this book.

CHILE

The most common types of business organizations operating in Chile are

i.*sociedades de responsabilidad limitada* (SRL), or **Limited Liability Companies/Partnerships;**

ii.*sociedades anónimas* (SA), or **Stock Corporations or Corporations;**

iii.*sociedades por acciones* (SPA), or **Simplified Corporations;**

iv.**Branches of Foreign Entities**.

Limited Liability Company (*Sociedad de Responsabilidad Limitada* or SRL) - This type of company primarily falls under the regulatory framework of Law No. 3.918. However, it is also subject to the rules that are applicable to general partnerships, and it must adhere to specific regulations found in the Commerce and Civil Codes. The liability of the members of an SRL is limited to the amount of their contributions or to the higher amount established in the bylaws. Equity rights can only be transferred with the unanimous approval of the partners. There is great flexibility as to the rules that may be included in the bylaws. The SRL is managed as established in the bylaws. If the bylaws do not state who manages the company, management corresponds to partners, by themselves or by representatives. If a manager is not appointed, all partners may administrate the company. Bylaws may establish different management options, such as appointing certain partner/s, third parties, or even a board of directors.

Corporation (Sociedad Anónima or S.A.) - This type of company is mainly regulated by Law No. 18,046 (the Corporations Act) as well as by the Corporations Regulations (Reglamento de Sociedades

Anónimas). A corporation may be open (public), closed (private), or special. Open corporations are those that register, voluntarily or by legal obligation, their shares in the Securities Registry and are under the control of the Financial Market Commission (Comisión para el Mercado Financiero or CMF). Special corporations (e.g., banks and insurance companies) are expressly established by law. Closed corporations are those that do not qualify as open or special. Its share capital is divided into shares, which may be transferred without limitation, except for certain exceptions such as those contained in shareholders' agreements. In private corporations, bylaws may establish certain restrictions, but this is not allowed in public corporations. The liability of shareholders is limited to the amount of their capital contributions and is managed by a board of directors appointed by the shareholders. The board is responsible for the administration and representation of the company and is entitled to delegate part of its powers to the CEO and other officers. A director's term of appointment, which is set forth in the bylaws, cannot exceed three years. Directors may also be re-elected indefinitely.

Simplified Corporation (Sociedades por Acciones or SpA) - Simplified corporations are regulated by special rules contained in the Commerce Code. They are also ruled by their bylaws and by the private corporations' rules in a suppletory manner. Unlike corporations, SpAs may be incorporated and operate with only one shareholder. The capital is divided into shares. Legal regulation for simplified corporations is more flexible than that of corporations as it allows special agreements regarding, for example, management, profit distributions, share ownership, multiple votes, and restrictions to voting rights. Management is flexible. Bylaws may establish different management options, such as appointing certain shareholder(s), third parties (or a board of directors. It is customary for simplified corporations to be managed by an administrator – usually the shareholder – who may act personally and/or through 1 or more agents and/or managers.

Branch of a Foreign Legal Entity (Agencia) - A branch acts as an alternative form of an entity as it corresponds to the presence of a foreign company (i.e., parent) in Chile that does not seek to incorporate a new company but instead only establishes a branch of the existing company. It is not a separate legal entity, except in the case of specific tax purposes.

The parent company is ruled by its local laws. The Commerce Code and the Corporations Act have certain special rules about the establishment and amendments of the branch for foreign companies and for-profit entities and corporations, respectively. It is managed by an agent appointed by the parent. The parent grants the agent extensive power to act on its behalf in Chile. This power shall expressly mention that the agent acts in Chile under the direct responsibility of the parent.

CHINA

Independent legal entity- Companies set up by or with foreign investors need to follow the general company law (and partnership law as applicable) pursuant to the new Foreign Investment Law, which took effect on January 1, 2020.

Therefore, depending on the foreign shareholding ratio in a limited liability company (LLC) or a company limited by shares as discussed below, it would still work to make reference to a wholly foreign-owned enterprise (WFOE) or a Sino-foreign joint venture enterprise in an economic sense.

However, a WFOE or JV, including an equity joint venture (EJV) or contractual joint venture (CJV), would no longer exist as a legal form.

All foreign-invested enterprises (FIEs) in China will take the legal structure of either a company (LLC or company listed by shares) or a partnership.

Limited Liability Company (LLC) - Managed by a board of directors or a single executive director (usually adopted by LLCs with a limited number of shareholders and relatively small size of operation), responsible for making major business decisions and overseeing general operations of an LLC.

The highest authority of an LLC is the shareholders' meeting. The director or the executive director is appointed/elected by the shareholder(s) of an LLC. Senior management officers run the day-to-day operations of an LLC, led by a general manager who is usually appointed by the board of directors or executive director.

Company Limited by Shares - This is an Independent legal entity. The board of directors has overall management responsibility, making major business decisions and overseeing the general operations of a company. The shareholders' assembly is the highest authority of a company listed by shares. The director is appointed/elected by the shareholders of a company. Senior management officers run the day-to-day operations of a company limited by shares, led by a general manager who is usually appointed by the board of directors.

Partnership Enterprise – This is NOT a separate legal person entity. A partnership agreement sets forth how the business is to be managed; one or several general partners can be designated to manage the business.

COLOMBIA

Under Colombian law, there are five types of commercial entities that can be incorporated:

General Partnership (Sociedad Colectiva) - Partners have subsidiary personal liability; the partnership board is the highest corporate body. A minimum of 2 partners is required at all times.

General Partnerships are closed companies where partners must manage the company themselves or unanimously authorize a third person to do so, as well as unanimously authorize the total or partial assignment of participation in the company or the possibility for partners to carry out similar lines of business on their own.

Limited Partnership (Sociedad en Comandita Simple por Acciones) - A hybrid type of company where partners can either be managing partners or limited partners. Each type of partner has different levels of liability, functions, voting rights, and participation in the company. There are also two types of limited partnerships under Colombian law. The simple limited partnership, where the partner's contributions are established as participation quota, and the share limited partnership, where the partner's contributions are established as shares.

Limited Liability Company (Sociedad de Responsabilidad Limitada) - The limited liability company is a hybrid type of company where partners can limit their responsibility to the amount of their contributions as a general rule. However, there are certain exceptions, such as responsibility regarding taxation and labor regulation or if such extended responsibility is included in the company's bylaws. Limited liability companies must have a minimum of 2 partners and a maximum of 25.

Corporation (Sociedad Anónima) - Shareholders have no personal liability. A corporation must have the Shareholders General Assembly as the highest corporate body, a board of directors, a legal representative designated by the board of directors, and a statutory auditor. A minimum of 5 shareholders is required, and it is generally used for large enterprises or financial institutions that are subject to the control and surveillance of the Colombian Superintendence of Finance.

Simplified Stock Company (Sociedad por Acciones Simplificada) - It is the most recent and flexible type of commercial entity created under Colombian legislation.

Shareholders have no personal liability. A simplified stock company must have a Shareholders General Assembly as the highest corporate body and a legal representative.

It can have a board of directors if shareholders require it. A minimum of one shareholder is required, and there is no maximum requirement.

CZECH REPUBLIC

Unlimited Partnership (veřejná obchodní společnost, v.o.s.) - A company in which at least two partners run their business under a common business name and are liable for all the partnership's debts to the full extent of their assets. The company does not need to have any registered capital. Monetary contributions of the shareholders to the company are voluntary. Each partner has a right to manage a partnership within the guidelines agreed upon by partners. One or more partners may, however, be entrusted with management responsibilities. All decisions are made jointly by all partners unless articles of association stipulate that a majority vote is sufficient. Transfer of ownership interest is currently forbidden.

Limited Partnership (komanditni spolecnost, k.s.) - It is a company with one or more partners that are liable for the debts of the company to the full extent of their assets (unlimited partners), and one or more partners that are liable for the debts of the company up to the number of their unpaid capital contributions (limited partners).

A limited partner must contribute to the registered capital of a company in the amount provided for in the partnership contract. Unlike unlimited partners, limited partners can transfer their ownership interests. The limited partner must provide a monetary contribution.

Limited Liability Company (spolecnost s rucenim omezenym, s.r.o./spol. s r.o.) - Separate and distinct legal entity. They are managed by one or more managing directors, who are responsible for making major business decisions and overseeing a corporation's general affairs as well as a stock corporation's day-to-day operations. It is one of the most common types of companies in the Czech Republic. Registered capital consists of contributions by shareholders who are jointly and severally liable for a company's debts up to the sum of their unpaid contribution to the registered capital. The company is responsible for its debts to the full extent of its assets. A supervisory board may also be established; however, it is not mandatory.

Joint Stock Company (akciova spolecnost, a.s.) - Separate and distinct legal entity. Registered capital consists of shares with a certain nominal value. It is liable for its debts to the full extent of its assets.

The governance system may be two-tier with a board of directors (predstavenstvo) and supervisory board (dozorci rada), or single-tier with an administrative board (správní rada). The company may issue registered or bearer shares. Bearer shares can be, however, issued only as dematerialized shares registered by the securities depository.

DENMARK

Limited Liability Company (Kapitalselskab) - There are three types of limited companies: public limited companies, private limited companies, and limited partnership companies. They are all separate and distinct legal entities. A limited liability company is owned by the shareholders, and the shareholders' meeting is the ultimate authority of the company.

However, the shareholders mainly control the company by instructing and supervising the board of directors and/or the general manager. In general, only the company is liable to creditors for corporate debts, and once the share contribution has been paid, the shareholders have no obligation to contribute further to the capital of the company.

EGYPT

Joint Stock Company (JSC) - A separate legal entity that may be a private company or a public company. It may offer its shares to public subscription, issue bonds and convertible securities, and offer them to the public.

The name of a JSC must derive from its purpose and may include the name(s) of any of its shareholders. Generally, there are no restrictions on foreign ownership, and the JSC may be wholly owned by foreigners, except for companies operating in Sinai (see below) and companies engaging in activities that are restricted by law for foreigners to participate in, such as Commercial agency, which requires the company to be wholly owned by Egyptians or persons who have acquired and held Egyptian nationality for at least ten years, importation activities for trading purposes, which requires that 51 percent of the shareholders must be Egyptians and acquiring land and/or real estate in Sinaix, which requires that Egyptians wholly own the company.

A company operating in Sinai must be established in the form of a JSC; 55 percent of its shareholders must be Egyptians, and it is subject to certain approval requirements. However, the foreign ownership restriction (i.e., the requirement that 55 percent of the shareholders be Egyptians) may be waived for companies that conduct the implementation of integrated development projects in Sinai, provided that the company has obtained a presidential decree, the required cabinet approval and any required approval of the competent local authorities.

It is managed by a minimum of three board members appointed by the general assembly.

The Board of Directors is responsible for the company's management and performing the required activities to achieve its purpose. It may delegate powers to one or more of its members in order to conduct certain act(s) and oversee certain aspects of the company, exercise some of the Board of Directors' powers and competencies, and undertake the actual management of the company.

All foreign Board of Directors members must pass a security clearance, but the company can generally be incorporated and conduct business even before such security clearance has been obtained, provided that it has submitted a completed application that is pending approval. However, by way of exception, board members of certain foreign nationalities (routinely subject to change) require the security clearance to be issued prior to starting the entity's business. Foreign employees cannot exceed 10 percent of all employees of the JSC.

Limited Liability Company (LLC) - A separate legal entity that is a private company, and its quotas cannot be listed or traded on any stock exchange. An LLC may not issue bonds or other financial debentures that are offered to the public. Quota holders appoint one or more managers to manage the LLC. The manager(s) may act individually or jointly in accordance with the terms of the LLC's Articles of Incorporation (AoI). Juridical persons may not be appointed as managers of an LLC.

One-Person Company (OPC) - It is newly introduced to the Egyptian market (Law No. 4 of 2018 amending the Companies Law) and formed by a sole founder, who can be either a natural or a juridical person. An OPC's equity cannot be listed or traded on any stock exchange. An OPC cannot issue bonds or other financial debentures that are offered to the public. Similarly, to a JSC and LLC, there are generally no restrictions on foreign ownership except for activities that foreigners are prohibited from participating in (e.g., commercial agency, importation activities for trading purposes, and acquiring land and/or real estate in Sinai). It is managed through the founder (i.e., sole proprietor) of the company or one or more appointed manager(s). Companies Law states that the rules governing the LLC are applicable to an OPC unless otherwise provided.

JSC, LLC, and OPC are collectively called "corporate entities" or "corporations" in some provisions in this book. Corporate entities are subject to the Companies Law. The Companies Law regulates, inter alia, the operations of the company's corporate bodies, such as the board of directors/managers, the general assembly, and the matters related to the management and control of the company. Further, depending on the type of activities undertaken, corporate entities may be established under Investment Law No. 72 of 2017 and Executive Regulations No. 2310 of 2017 (the Investment Law). In such cases, the Companies Law would apply to the extent that the Investment Law is silent to a certain matter. There are other entity types in Egypt, but the ones listed above are the most commonly used.

Branch of a Foreign Corporation (Branch) - Not a separate legal entity. Foreign corporations can conduct business in Egypt via a local branch. A foreign-based company (i.e., parent company) can establish a branch in Egypt by registering with the General Authority for Investment and Free Zones (GAFI) as a foreign company carrying on business in Egypt. A branch must be formed for the purpose of implementing specific public or private sector agreements in Egypt. One or more branch managers, whether Egyptian or foreign, must be appointed to run the business activities in Egypt. The business name must be the name of a foreign-based company.

Representative Office - Not a separate legal entity. It can only be used for studying the feasibility of production or carrying out market surveys. Cannot engage in any commercial activities or execute agreements with third parties on behalf of a foreign company.

FINLAND

Limited Liability Company (Osakeyhtiö, Oy) - Separate and distinct legal entity. They are managed by a board of directors, which is responsible for making major business decisions and overseeing the general affairs of the company. Directors are elected by the shareholders of the Oy. The managing director (optional), who runs the day-to-day operations of the Oy, is appointed by the board of directors. Other officers are appointed by the board of directors or by the managing director.

FRANCE

Société par actions simplifiée (SAS) - The SAS is an increasingly used type of company, mainly because of its great flexibility and low capital requirements. The SAS is a more flexible corporate form than the SARL, which is a more binding vehicle. The SAS is essentially a simplified form of the SA. It has a number of advantages due to its flexibility such as - the law does not impose a particular management structure for the SAS; the president is the only compulsory corporate body; there is greater freedom for organizing the management and operating structures of a SAS. The SAS does not have access to the capital markets and its shares cannot be listed on a stock exchange.

Société à responsabilité limitée (SARL) - Easy to set up and operate. Relevant for small businesses. One or more directors must not be corporate entities but do not need to be shareholders. The SARL is a widely utilized form of corporation in France, mainly due to the number of advantages it offers to small businesses, such as low capital requirements and simple rules and regulations. It is more restrictive and less flexible than the SAS. Sweat equity permitted: a shareholder offers the company his time, work, and professional knowledge (does not contribute to forming the capital but has the right to shares in the company, share of profits, and participation in collective decisions). The SARL does not have access to the capital markets, and its shares cannot be listed on a stock exchange.

Société anonyme (SA) - The SA is a historical legal form mainly used by large corporations in France, as it enables the public offering of shares. Tailored for large companies needing external capital by resorting to the market, it is a very complex form of company, not commonly appropriate for first incorporation in France.

Branch of a Foreign Company - Under French law, an entity operating in France shall register with the French Registry of Commerce and Companies (RCS) only if it is conducting a "commercial activity." A foreign company is only required to register with the local Registry of Commerce and Companies when its operations in France constitute a permanent establishment, where an autonomous activity (as opposed to "preparatory and auxiliary" activities) is being conducted and managed by an agent of the foreign company or a person who may bind the foreign company vis-à-vis third parties. Under French law, the branch is a direct form of implantation in France of a foreign company. A branch is not a separate legal entity and is therefore deemed to be the same legal entity as the foreign company, which remains solely responsible for the operation of its branch in France.

The main difference between a French branch and a French subsidiary is that a branch is a mere emanation of the parent company in France, with no legal existence or distinct assets or liabilities, and a subsidiary is an independent entity with its own legal existence, bylaws, and capital contributions. As a consequence, the parent company has unlimited liability for any debts and liabilities incurred by the branch in France. It has limited liability for the debts and liabilities incurred by its subsidiary (provided that the subsidiary is not incorporated under the form of a partnership, i.e., SNC or civil company) in case it becomes insolvent (i.e., limited to its initial capital contribution and the amount of any shareholder's loan which cannot be reimbursed within the context of a liquidation due to insufficiency of assets).

GERMANY

GMBH – Limited Liability Company - The GmbH is a company for all kinds of business with a corporate organization and its own legal personality. The shareholders mainly control the company by instructing the managing directors. It has a share capital, which matches the total of the share contributions to be made by the shareholders.

Only the company is liable to creditors for corporate debts. The legal frame allows individual formation to a certain extent.

GREECE

Societe Anonyme (S.A.) - A societe anonyme is a legal entity where liability can be imposed solely on its assets and not personally on its shareholders. A societe anonyme is a company managed by its general meeting of shareholders and its board of directors. The board of directors is competent to decide on every act concerning the management of the company, the administration of its assets, and the pursuit of the company's business activities in general. Directors are elected by the shareholders of the company. Officers who run the company's day-to-day operations are appointed by directors.

Limited Liability Company (L.T.D.) and Private Company (P.C.) - Separate and distinct legal entity. Shareholder (partner) liability is limited solely to the assets of the company. The governing body of the company is the partners' meeting (assembly), which is responsible for making major business decisions and overseeing the general affairs of the company. The director (administrator) of the company is elected by the company's partners and is the legal representative responsible for managing the company's day-to-day operations and business.

HONG KONG, SAR

Limited Private Companies - Separate and distinct legal entity. They are managed by a board of directors, which is responsible for making major business decisions and overseeing the general affairs of the corporation. Directors are elected by the shareholders or the board of the corporation. Officers could be appointed by directors to run the day-to-day operations of the corporation.

HUNGARY

Private Company Limited By Shares (Zrt.) - A private company limited by shares (zártkörűen működő részvénytársaság or Zrt.) is a separate and distinct legal entity. A Zrt. is established with a predetermined amount of share capital. Such share capital is represented by shares with a face (par or nominal) value. The shares may be issued either as printed shares or dematerialized (i.e., e-shares registered on a securities/investment account). The owners of a Zrt. are the shareholders.

The liability of the shareholders is limited to their respective share capital contributions and managed by a board of directors, which is responsible for making major business decisions and overseeing the general affairs of the Zrt. Shareholders may also decide to appoint a single director instead of a board to perform the duties of the board of directors.

Directors are elected by shareholders of a Zrt. Company managers (who must be employees of the company) may also be appointed by shareholders to assist the directors in day-to-day operations.

Limited Liability Company (Kft.) - A limited liability company (korlátolt felelősségű társaság or Kft.) is a separate and distinct legal entity. A Kft. is established with a predetermined amount of initial capital provided by its quota holders.

The equity contribution of such quota holders is not – and must not be – embodied in any negotiable instrument (e.g., share certificate). Liability of the quota holders is limited to their capital contributions and managed by managing directors appointed by quota holders.

Shareholders may also decide to set up a board of directors instead of appointing one or more individual managing directors. Company managers (who must be employees of the company) may also be appointed by quota holders to assist managing directors in the day-to-day operations of the firm.

INDONESIA

Limited Liability Company - It is a separate and distinct legal entity, managed by the board of directors, responsible for making major business decisions and overseeing the general affairs of the company under the supervision of a board of commissioners. The members of the Board of Directors and the Board of Commissioners are appointed and dismissed by the general meeting of shareholders.

IRELAND

The information in this guide provides a summary of 2 corporate structures that are commonly used in Ireland. Other alternatives, such as a designated activity company (DAC), a private unlimited company (ULC), a company limited by guarantee (CLG), or a public limited company (PLC), could be useful in some instances but are less common.

Private Company Limited by Shares (LTD) - Separate and distinct legal entity. They are managed by a board of directors, which has collective authority and is responsible for managing the affairs of the company. Subject to the constitution, the shareholders have the power to appoint and remove directors. An LTD cannot offer shares to the public, and the company's constitution generally restricts the right to transfer shares. Shareholders have limited liability protection.

External Company - A company with limited liability incorporated under the laws of another jurisdiction and establishing operations in Ireland is obliged to register as an external company (i.e., a branch) in certain circumstances.

The requirement to register a branch generally arises where the Irish operations of the foreign company have a physical place of business, the appearance of permanency, a person to manage the place of business, and the authority to negotiate and contract directly with third parties on an independent basis. From an Irish perspective, the branch is not a separate legal entity from the "home" or "parent" company.

ITALY

Società a responsabilità limitata (S.R.L.) - Separate and distinct legal entity. An S.r.l. can be managed by a sole director or a board of directors composed of two or more members or two or more directors acting jointly or severally.

Directors can also be quota-holders. Directors are elected by the quota-holders with a proper decision.

JAPAN

Registered Branch - This form is often used by foreign companies seeking to gain a presence and do business in Japan without establishing a subsidiary. A foreign company must appoint at least one representative in Japan.

Kabushiki-Kaisha (KK) - A KK is a distinct legal entity. KKs are most similar to C-corporations in other jurisdictions. The liability for shareholders is limited, and the KK is a well-established structure. The KK may be established with or without a board of directors.

Godo-Kaisha (GK) - A GK structure is similar to an LLC in other jurisdictions. The GK allows more flexibility in regard to corporate governance and management decisions. The annual corporate governance requirements costs are generally lower as there are few formal corporate governance requirements that must be observed.

LUXEMBOURG

Private Limited Liability Company (*Société à responsabilité limitée* or S.à r.l.) - Separate and distinct legal personality. They are handled by a manager or a board of managers (collège de gérance) – who may or may not be shareholders - responsible for making major business decisions and overseeing the general affairs of the company.

Managers are elected by the shareholders for a limited or unlimited term and represent the company acting alone or as set out in the articles of incorporation/association if more than one manager has been appointed.

Public Limited Liability Company (Société Anonyme or S.A.) - Separate and distinct legal personality. An SA may be organized as a 1-tier company (i.e., managed by a sole director or a board of directors composed of at least three directors) or a 2-tier company (i.e., an executive board (directoire) and a supervisory board (conseil de surveillance). Directors are elected by the shareholders and represent the company acting alone or as set out in the articles of incorporation/association if more than one director has been appointed.

Special Limited Partnership (Société en commandite spéciale or SCSp) - Largely inspired by the Anglo-Saxon limited partnership regimes, the special limited partnership has been designed to bolster Luxembourg's position as the main alternative investment fund structuring hub in the EU at a time when the manager regulation is seen as a potential substitute for product regulation.

With no legal personality, the SCSp is formed by written agreement – a limited partnership agreement – for a limited or unlimited duration, between 1 or more general partner(s) (associés commandités) jointly and severally liable for the partnership's commitments and one or more limited partner(s) (associés commanditaires) whose liability does not extend beyond their commitment. A high level of contractual freedom and structuring flexibility characterize the SCSp as most of the relevant provisions applicable to the SCSp may be contractually outlined in the limited partnership agreement.

MALAYSIA

The first step to starting a business in Malaysia is to set up a business entity with the Companies Commission of Malaysia. There are two types of business entities: the unincorporated entity and the incorporated separate legal entity. The unincorporated entities are **Sole Proprietorship and Partnership.**

A sole proprietorship is an entity with one person, whereas a partnership is a business entity that is owned by at least two persons but not more than 20 persons.

Both the sole proprietorship and partnership do not constitute separate legal entities, and the business partners can sue and be sued in their personal names.

A business owner or partners are exposed to personal risks and liabilities. The incorporated separate legal entities are companies limited by shares or private limited companies.

A company is limited by guarantee, unlimited company, and limited liability partnership. Private limited companies are the most established business entities as the shareholders of private limited companies are not exposed to personal risks and liabilities; their liabilities are limited to the number of shares that they own.

MAURITIUS

There are different types of entities to conduct business in or from Mauritius and the most common types **are Company Limited By Shares, Company Limited By Guarantee, Company Limited By Shares and By Guarantee, Unlimited Company, Foreign Company, Limited Life Company (Constitutionally Limited Life Not Exceeding 50 Years), Global Business Corporation, Authorized Company, Protected Cell Company, Société, Trust, Foundations, Limited Liability Partnerships and Variable Capital Company.** Companies are categorized between private companies and public companies. The most common type of company is the private company limited by shares, which is governed by the Companies Act 2001 of Mauritius (the Companies Act). Global Business Corporations, Authorized Companies, and Protected Cell Companies are also governed by the Companies Act. Any entity that proposes to conduct business outside of Mauritius must apply for a license (Global Business Corporation License or Authorized Company License) from the Financial Services Commission of Mauritius (FSC).

MEXICO

S.A. De C.V. - It is a separate legal entity independent from its shareholders. Two shareholders are required at all times. Shareholders' meetings are the supreme organ of the corporation. It is managed by a board of directors or a sole administrator, who is responsible for making major business decisions and overseeing the general affairs of the corporation. Directors are elected by the shareholders of the corporation. Officers who run the day-to-day operations of the corporation are appointed by the directors or the shareholders' meeting.

S. De R.L. De C.V. - It is a separate legal entity independent from its partners. Two partners are required at all times. Partners' meetings are the supreme organ of the company. It is managed by a board of directors or a sole administrator, who is responsible for making major business decisions and overseeing the general affairs of the company.

Directors are elected by the partners of the company. Officers who run the day-to-day operations of the company are appointed by the directors or the partners' meeting.

S.A.P.I. De C.V. - it is a separate legal entity, independent from its shareholders. Two shareholders are required at all times. Shareholders' meetings are the supreme organ of the corporation. It is managed by a board of directors, which is responsible for making major business decisions and overseeing the general affairs of the corporation.

Directors are elected by the shareholders of the corporation. Officers who run the day-to-day operations of the corporation are appointed by the directors or the shareholders' meeting.

NETHERLANDS

Branch Office - Not a separate legal entity. A branch office is a local office of a non-Dutch legal entity in the Netherlands (the head office).

B.V. (Private Company with Limited Liability) - It is a separate and distinct legal entity. They are managed by a board of directors, which is responsible for making major business decisions, overseeing the general affairs, and running the day-to-day operations of the BV. Directors are appointed by the shareholders of the BV.

A BV can have a supervisory board to supervise the policies of the board of directors and the general course of affairs of the BV and its affiliated business. It is also possible to create a so-called 1-tier board consisting of executive and non-executive directors.

Co-Operative U.A. - It is a separate and distinct legal entity. They are managed by a management board, which is responsible for making major business decisions, overseeing the general affairs, and running the day-to-day operations of the co-operative. Directors are appointed by the members of the co-operative. A co-operative can have a supervisory board to supervise the policies of the management board and the general course of affairs of the co-operative and its affiliated business. It is also possible to create a so-called 1-tier board consisting of executive and non-executive directors.

C.V. (A Limited Partnership) - A CV is not a legal entity under Dutch law. It is a partnership agreement between 1 or more general partners and one or more limited partners. The general partner has overall management and day-to-day responsibility. The partnership agreement can provide for the possibility that the partners elect a management committee, which will manage the everyday business activities of the CV and carry out the business and activities of the CV on behalf of the general partner in accordance with the power granted to them by the general partner.

NEW ZEALAND

Limited Liability Companies - Limited liability companies incorporated in accordance with the Companies Act 1993 **(Companies Act)** are the most common corporate structure used in New Zealand. Limited liability companies generally limit the liability of shareholders, except:

i. To the extent of any amount unpaid on a share held by a shareholder.

ii. As provided for under that company's constitution.

iii. For other specific exceptions as set out in the Companies Act.

The board of directors generally manages and supervises the conduct of business and the general affairs of companies (which, subject to certain limitations, may be delegated to a committee). Directors are generally appointed by way of ordinary resolution of a company's shareholders but can also be appointed by the Board, where the constitution or other governing document (as may be applicable) expressly provides a power of appointment.

Limited liability companies with 50 or more shareholders (and 50 or more share parcels) and assets of at least NZD30 million (including the assets of their respective subsidiaries) or revenue of at least NZD15 million (including the revenue of their subsidiaries) are "code companies" for the purposes of the Takeover Regulations 2000 and the Takeovers Code.

Code companies are subject to the provisions of the Takeovers Code. They are subject to strict requirements when shareholders (including their respective associates) hold 20 percent or more of the shares on issue and that shareholder wishes to increase its shareholding in the code company. Limited liability companies that wish to list on a licensed market operated by NZX Limited, including the NZX, will be subject to the relevant listing rules and other legislative requirements (including the Companies Act and the NZX listing rules) and will also be considered code companies under the Takeovers Code. There is no limit on public companies' ability to raise funds from the public (either through an initial public offer – or IPO – or through a post-listing capital raise or rights issue), provided that the various disclosure requirements and other statutory rules are complied with, including those set out in the Financial Markets Conduct Act 2013 (FMCA).

Branch - Overseas companies "carrying on business" in New Zealand must register as a branch of an overseas company with the

New Zealand Companies Office (Companies Office). The Companies Office is a government agency in New Zealand that provides business registry services in relation to corporate entities, personal property, and capital market securities.

The term "carrying on business" is not explicitly defined in New Zealand law. However, it typically includes businesses with employees in New Zealand, those that maintain an office or business premises in New Zealand, or those that regularly engage in business transactions within the country. For this reason, it is advisable that foreign companies seek professional advice before commencing business in New Zealand to ensure compliance with New Zealand law.

NIGERIA

The vehicles through which a business may be set up and conducted in Nigeria are Company limited by shares **(Private/Public Company),** Unlimited company (private/public), Company limited by guarantee, Limited liability partnership, Limited partnership, Business names incorporated, and Trustees.

NORWAY

Private limited liability companies (private LLCs) - Separate and distinct legal entities managed by a board of directors, which is responsible for making major business decisions. The board of directors also has a supervisory function in relation to the company's activities and the executive managers of the company. Directors are elected by the shareholders of the company.

Employees may have the right to appoint a minority of the board members if the number of employees exceeds certain thresholds. The day-to-day operations of the company are usually carried out by the general manager, who is appointed by the board of directors.

However, private LLCs are not obligated to have a general manager. If no general manager is appointed, the chairman of the board of directors is responsible for the day-to-day management. The shareholders of the company constitute the general meeting, which is the superior body of the company.

Public Limited Liability Companies (public LLCs) - Separate and distinct legal entities. The governmental structure of public LLCs is unitary with private LLCs. Public LLCs must have a general manager who is responsible for the day-to-day management of the company. The general manager is appointed by the board of directors. Only public LLCs or other similar foreign companies can be listed on a regulated market.

Partnerships With Unlimited Liability - Separate and distinct legal entity managed by the partnership meeting. Partnership meetings can appoint a board of directors and a general manager to manage the company and handle the day-to-day responsibilities.

PERU

The most common types of business organizations operating in Peru are

    i. *Sociedades Anónimas* (S.A.), Or Stock Corporations;
    ii. *Sociedades De Responsabilidad Limitada* (S.R.L.), Or Limited Liability Companies/Partnerships; And,
    iii. Branches of Foreign Entities.

Corporation (*Sociedad Anónima* or S.A.) - This type of company is mainly regulated by the Corporations Act, as well as by the Corporations' Registry Regulations (Reglamento del Registro de Sociedades). A corporation may be open (public), in which case it would be a sociedad anónima abierta (S.A.A.) or private, in which case it could be (i) a closed stock corporation or sociedad anónima cerrada (S.A.C.); or, (ii) a regular corporation or sociedad anónima

215

(S.A.). Open corporations are those that register, voluntarily or by legal obligation, their shares in the Public Registry of the Securities Market of the Superintendency of the Securities Market (Registro Público del Mercado de Valores de la Superintendencia del Mercado de Valores) and are under the control of such Superintendency. Closed stock corporations are those incorporated as such and may not have more than 20 shareholders. Finally, corporations are those that do not qualify as open or closed. A corporation's share capital is divided into shares. In the case of open corporations, the shares may be transferred without limitation. Restrictions to shares' transfers regulated in their bylaws or in shareholders' agreements are not enforceable. On the contrary, a right of first refusal applies to closed stock corporations unless otherwise provided in their bylaws. In the case of regular corporations, the shares may be transferred without limitation, except if certain restrictions are established in their bylaws or in shareholders' agreements. The liability of shareholders is limited to the amount of their contributions to capital. Corporations (except for some closed stock corporations) are managed by a board of directors formed by -at least- 3 members appointed by the shareholders. The board is responsible for the administration and representation of the company and is entitled to delegate part of its powers to the CEO and other officers. A director's term of appointment, which is set forth in the bylaws, cannot be less than one year and shall not exceed three years. Directors may also be re-elected indefinitely. If the shareholders of a closed stock corporation decide so, such an entity could refrain from having a board of directors, in which case it would be managed by a CEO.

Limited Liability Company (Sociedad de Responsabilidad Limitada or S.R.L.) - This type of company is mainly regulated by the Corporations Act, as well as by the Corporations' Registry Regulations (Reglamento del Registro de Sociedades). The liability of the members of a S.R.L. is limited to the amount of their contributions. A right of first refusal shall always be applicable, and equity rights may only be transferred by virtue of a public deed that shall be recorded before the Public Registry of the domicile of the corresponding entity. There is great flexibility as to the rules that may be included in the bylaws. The management of an S.R.L. is entrusted to one or more managers (whether partners or not), who shall represent it in all matters relating to its company purpose. The managers are prohibited from engaging (for their own account or for the account of others) in the same type of business that corresponds to the company's purpose.

Branch of a Foreign Legal Entity (Sucursal) - A branch acts as an alternative form of entity, as it corresponds to the presence of a foreign company (the parent company) in Peru that does not seek to incorporate a new company, but instead only establishes a branch of the existing company. It is not a separate legal entity except for tax purposes. The parent company is ruled by its local laws but shall comply with the applicable Peruvian legislation regarding the obligations undertaken by the branch in Peru. The Corporations Act contains certain special rules regarding the establishment (and amendments) of a branch by foreign companies. A branch is managed by a permanent legal representative appointed by the parent company.

PHILIPPINES

Subsidiary - A subsidiary is a domestic stock corporation, either wholly or partially owned (but controlled) by a foreign corporation. It has a separate and distinct legal entity from its parent. It is managed by its board of directors, which exercises all corporate powers, conducts all business, and controls all property of the corporation. Directors are elected by the stockholders themselves. Officers are elected by the directors, and they perform the duties imposed on them by law and the bylaws of the corporation.

Branch office - It is an extension of, and not a separate and distinct entity from, the foreign corporation. It carries out business activities of the head office and derives income from the Philippines. A resident agent is designated to whom summons and other legal processes may be served on behalf of the foreign corporation.

Representative Office - It is an extension of, and not a separate and distinct entity from, the foreign corporation. It deals directly with the clients of the head office in the Philippines but does not derive income from the country and is fully subsidized by its head office. A resident agent is appointed to receive summons and other legal documents on behalf of the foreign corporation.

Regional or Area Headquarters - It is an administrative branch of a multinational company and, thus, not a separate and distinct legal entity. It is established to supervise, communicate, and coordinate the multinational company's subsidiaries, affiliates, and branches in the Asia-Pacific region. It is not allowed to do business or derive any income from sources within the Philippines. Its operations must be fully subsidized through inward remittances from its head office.

Regional Operating Headquarters - It is an administrative branch of a multinational company and, thus, not a separate and distinct legal entity. It is established to perform qualifying services to the multinational company's affiliates, subsidiaries, or branches in the Philippines, the Asia-Pacific region, and other foreign markets. It is prohibited from offering its services to entities other than the foregoing. It is also prohibited, directly or indirectly, to solicit or market goods and services on behalf of the multinational company or any of its affiliates or subsidiaries. It is allowed to derive income from sources within the Philippines.

Partnership - A partnership has a legal personality separate and distinct from its partners. Generally, each partner is considered an agent of the partnership, and their acts are binding unless otherwise provided in the articles of partnership. A foreign corporation may be a partner in a domestic partnership only after such a foreign corporation obtains a license to transact business in the Philippines.

One Person Corporation - The Revised Corporation Code (RCC) introduced the new concept of a One Person Corporation (OPC), which is defined as "a corporation with a single stockholder." This corporation may only be formed by a natural person, trust, or an estate. Banks and quasi-banks, trust, insurance, public and publicly listed companies, and non-chartered government-owned and - controlled corporations are not allowed to incorporate as OPCs. Further, a natural person licensed to exercise a profession is also generally not allowed to organize as an OPC for the purpose of exercising such profession, except as otherwise provided under special laws. Similar to ordinary corporations, an OPC has no minimum capital stock requirement. Unlike an ordinary corporation, an OPC is not required to submit corporate bylaws. The single stockholder serves as the sole director and president of the OPC. The OPC is required to appoint a treasurer, corporate secretary, and other officers as necessary within 15 days from the issuance of its certificate of incorporation. However, the single stockholder is proscribed from being appointed as the corporate secretary. The single stockholder is required to designate a nominee and an alternate nominee who shall take their place as director in the event of their death or incapacity. The extent and limitations of the authority of the nominee and alternate nominee shall be stated in the articles of incorporation. The nominee and alternate nominee may be changed at any time and without the need for amendment of the articles of incorporation. In case of death or permanent incapacity, the nominee shall sit as director only until the legal heirs of the single stockholder have been lawfully determined, and the heirs have designated one of them or have agreed that the estate shall be the single stockholder. In lieu of meetings, a written resolution signed and dated by the single stockholder and recorded in the minute's book shall be sufficient when action is needed on any matter.

Aside from the minutes book, the OPC shall also be required to submit reportorial requirements. Failure to submit such requirements three times within a period of 5 years may place the

OPC under delinquent status. The reportorial requirements are annual financial statements, a report containing explanations or comments by the president on every qualification, reservation, or adverse remark or disclaimer made by the auditor in the latter's report, a disclosure of all self-dealings and related party transactions and other reports required by the SEC. The RCC allows the conversion from an ordinary corporation to an OPC and from an OPC to an ordinary stock corporation. An ordinary stock corporation may be converted to an OPC when the single stockholder acquires all the stocks of an ordinary stock corporation and files an application for conversion with the SEC. An OPC may be converted into an ordinary stock corporation after due notice to the SEC of such fact and of the circumstances leading to the conversion. One such circumstance provided by the law is the death of a single stockholder. In such a case, the legal heirs may decide to either wind up or dissolve the OPC or convert it into an ordinary stock corporation.

POLAND

Foreign companies can conduct business activity in Poland in forms similar to those that can be found in other European countries. These include Commercial companies (limited liability companies and joint-stock companies, in the future also simplified joint-stock companies), Partnerships (general partnerships, professional partnerships, limited partnerships, and limited joint-stock partnerships), Branch offices of foreign companies, and Representative offices of foreign companies.

PORTUGAL

Portuguese law provides for various types of companies, two of which are most commonly used: Limited liability companies by shares (S.A. or Sociedade Anónima) and Limited liability companies by quota (or Sociedade por Quotas).

LDA. Companies - These companies are incorporated with at least two shareholders. There is also a sub-type of company bearing one single shareholder, in this case, identified by the denomination Sociedade Unipessoal LDA. (sole shareholder company). However, an individual may only be the sole shareholder of 1 Sociedade Unipessoal. The share capital in these companies is divided into quotas. As a rule, and upon incorporation, each shareholder has one single quota, which nominal value may vary from EUR 1 to any given amount. Consequently, the minimum share capital of LDA companies is EUR 2, and for the Sociedade Unipessoal sub-type, the minimum share capital is EUR 1. Quotas are registered with the Commercial Registrar of Companies, do not have a physical existence, and cannot be listed on a Stock Exchange. LDA companies have a simplified governance structure, comprising the General Meeting (which in the case of a Sociedade Unipessoal is assured by the sole shareholder), one or more directors, and one accountant (TOC). Additionally, one Independent Auditor or a Supervisory Board is required for a period of 2 years if two of the following thresholds are met:

- Balance exceeds 5 million
- Total turnover and other revenue of at least EUR3 million
- Average number of 50 or more employees.

S.A. Companies - These companies are incorporated with at least 5 shareholders, except in cases where a company is the sole shareholder. The share capital is represented by shares which can have, or not, a nominal value. In the first case, all shares must have the same nominal value. The minimum nominal value – or, for shares with no nominal value, the minimum issue value – is of EUR 0.01. In any case, the minimum share capital required is EUR 50,000. Shares are nominative, and may be in book entry form, or titled, and are registered.

i. With the company, in a share ledger book,

ii. In a banking entity, or

iii. In a central registration entity. Governance structure is more complex than LDA. companies, and 3 different governance structures are available:

Portuguese "traditional" system:

    a) **General meeting:**

• 1 director (provided the share capital remains below EUR200,000), or a board of directors (more than 1 member and not necessarily in an odd number).

• Supervisory body, which may be:

• 1 Independent Auditor (plus their substitute; both must be chartered accountants or a chartered accountants' firm), or

• A supervisory board (minimum of 3 members plus 1 substitute; at least 1 of the effective members must be a chartered accountant or a chartered accountants' firm), plus a chartered accountant or a chartered accountant firm (mandatory for Stock Exchange listed companies).

    b) **2-tier system:**

• General meeting

• A 2-tier board structure comprising

• A general and supervisory board

• An executive board of directors or 1 executive director (provided the share capital remains below EUR 200,000)

• 1 independent auditor.

    c) **1-tier system:**

• General meeting

• A board of directors which includes an audit committee of no fewer than 3 members

• 1 independent auditor

- A company secretary (who must have an appropriate degree or be a paralegal) is only mandatory for Stock Exchange listed companies.

PUERTO RICO

Corporations - Corporations are entities whose liability is separate and distinct from that of their shareholders, directors, and officers. Corporations may be established for any lawful business purposes, with limited exceptions. They may be organized by individual(s) and/or legal entities by filing a certificate of incorporation at the Puerto Rico State Department. A corporation has the power to enter into contracts, hold property, and sue and be sued in its own name; it also has continuity of existence and free transferability of ownership interests. Generally, the certificate of incorporation grants the corporation legal existence as soon as it is filed with the Puerto Rico Secretary of State. Puerto Rico corporations must maintain a designated principal office and registered agent for the service of process in Puerto Rico.

Limited Liability Companies - Limited liability companies (LLCs) are becoming the preferred business method in Puerto Rico. Any natural or legal person may organize LLCs by filing articles of organization (also referred to as the certificate of formation) in the Puerto Rico State Department. LLCs offer their owners the same limited liability protection granted by law to corporations and the flexibility to manage their internal affairs as a partnership, corporation, or a combination of both in accordance with an LLC agreement (also referred to as an operating agreement), which typically governs the entity. LLCs are taxed by default as corporations and are subject to tax at both the business entity and shareholder levels. However, an LLC may elect to be treated as a partnership for tax purposes, receiving pass-through treatment by making an election on Form SC 6045 on or before the due date, including extensions, of the LLC's Puerto Rico income tax return for the taxable year in which the election is to become effective. The Secretary of the Puerto Rico Treasury Department may provide further guidance on the form and manner of making such an election. Puerto Rico limited liability companies, as is the case with corporations, must maintain a designated principal office and registered agent for service of process in Puerto Rico.

ROMANIA

Several types of companies may be used as corporate vehicles in Romania. Joint stock companies (societate pe actiuni or JSC) and limited liability companies (societate cu raspundere limitata or LLC) are the most commonly used, given their flexible incorporation procedure and limitation of the shareholders' liability.

Joint Stock Company (JSC) - It is a separate and distinct legal entity. A JSC may be managed by one or more directors (forming a board of directors), with the possibility of management delegation. In the 1-tier system, directors are appointed by the general meeting of shareholders, while managers are appointed by the board of directors or an executive board and a supervisory board. In the 2-tier system, members of the executive board are appointed by the supervisory board; the general meeting of shareholders appoints members of the supervisory board. Generally, if a JSC is managed in a 1-tier system, a sole director/board of directors represent(s) the company through its president. Under the 2-tier system, representation power is exercised by members of the executive board. Special provisions apply in the case of publicly listed companies.

Limited Liability Company (LLC) - It is a separate and distinct legal entity. An LLC may be managed by one or more directors appointed by the general meeting of shareholders. A company is represented by its directors.

RUSSIA

Joint-stock company (public and non-public)- A commercial organization with its charter capital divided into a specific number of shares. Shares qualify as securities under Russian law. The shareholders of the company are not liable for the obligations of the company and bear the risk of losses in connection with the company's activity within the cost of shares in their possession. The company is overseen by three key entities:

i.   The general shareholders' meeting (the highest governing body responsible for major decisions like charter amendments, reorganization, profit distribution, and annual report approval)
ii. The executive body (comprising a managing director or managing director and directorate) in charge of day-to-day operations
iii. The board of directors responsible for overall company affairs.

The company may also opt to have two or more managing directors who may act separately or jointly. In a company with less than 50 shareholders, the charter of the company may provide that the general shareholders' meeting shall carry out the functions of the company's board of directors.

Limited Liability Company- It is a commercial organization, the charter capital of which is divided into participatory interests. Participatory interests do not qualify as securities under Russian law. The company members are not liable for the obligations of the company and bear the risk of losses in connection with the company's activity within the cost of the contributions they have made. Managed by the general members' meeting, the highest management body of the company, which is responsible for major decisions regarding the company (e.g., amending the charter, reorganization, and liquidation, approving annual reports) by the executive body (i.e., the managing director or managing director and directorate), which is responsible for day-to-day activities of the company and, in some cases, by the board of directors, which is responsible for overseeing the general affairs of the company. The company may also opt to have two or more managing directors who may act separately or jointly.

SAUDI ARABIA

Limited Liability Company - A limited liability company is a popular corporate vehicle among foreign investors in Saudi Arabia. The personal liability for each of the partners/shareholders is limited to the individual partner's contribution to the company's share capital.

SINGAPORE

Limited Liability Company - Separate and distinct legal entity with limited liability for its members. The business of a company shall be managed by or under the direction or supervision of a board of directors, which is responsible for making major business decisions and overseeing the general affairs of the company. Appointment of directors is generally left to the company's constitution as the Companies Act 1967 of Singapore (CA) does not prescribe the manner in which directors are to be appointed, and they are typically nominated by the shareholders of the company. The favorable 1-tier corporate taxation regime proves to be advantageous to shareholders.

SOUTH AFRICA

In addition to doing business as a sole proprietor (where an individual conducts business in their personal capacity), there are different types of for-profit entities used to conduct business in South Africa:

- Private company
- Public company
- Personal liability company
- External company (these entities are branches of foreign companies and not South African incorporated entities as discussed below)
- Trust (unique legal arrangements where property is transferred to and held or administered by one or more trustees on behalf of the trust beneficiaries for their benefit or for the achievement of a specified purpose other than the trustees' own benefit)
- Partnership (regulated by a consensual contract between 2 or more persons to place their assets, labor and skill, or some or all of them, in lawful commerce or business, and to divide the profit and bear the loss in certain proportions)

SOUTH KOREA

Joint-Stock Company (*Jusik Hoesa*) - Separate and distinct entity. The general meeting of shareholders is the ultimate decision-making body. It determines the fundamental matters regarding the company's structure and management specified under the Korean Commercial Code (KCC) or the company's articles of incorporation (AOI). The board of directors, which is comprised of directors who are elected at the general meeting of shareholders, decides important matters related to the daily operations of the company not specially reserved for determination by the general meeting of shareholders under the KCC or the AOI.

The representative director or executive officer, who is elected by the board of directors, is the administrative arm responsible for implementing the decisions of the general meeting of shareholders and board of directors with authority to bind the company and Statutory auditor(s) supervise(s) the management of the company's business and audits the company's accounts.

Limited Company (Yuhan Hoesa) - A separate and distinct entity, the General meeting of members is the ultimate decision-making body and determines fundamental matters regarding the company's structure and management. Directors elected at the general meeting of members decide important matters related to the daily operations of the company not specially reserved for determination by the general meeting of members by a majority vote.

The director (in case a limited company has only one director) or representative director elected at the general meeting of members (in case a limited company has two or more directors) is the administrative arm responsible for implementing the decisions of the general members and directors with the authority to bind the company, and Statutory auditor(s) (if any) supervise(s) the management of the company's business and audits the company's accounts.

SPAIN

Branch (Sucursal) - Secondary establishment, subordinated to a headquarters, with permanent representation and a certain degree of autonomy, through which the principal company's business is totally or partially carried out. The board of directors of the headquarters will be competent to determine the creation of a branch as well as its cancelation or change of location.

Limited Liability Company (Sociedad Limitada) is a separate and distinct legal entity. It is managed by a board of directors, a sole director, joint directors, or joint and several directors.

The board of directors (or the relevant directors if there is no board) is responsible for making business decisions and overseeing the affairs of a company. Directors are appointed by shareholders of a company. Executive committee and managing directors are only appointed if there is a board of directors that requires delegation of board powers.

Joint-Stock Company (Sociedad Anónima) - Separate and distinct legal entity. It is managed by a board of directors, a sole director, joint directors, or joint and several directors.

The Board of Directors (or relevant directors if there is no board) is responsible for making business decisions and overseeing the affairs of a company.

Directors are elected by shareholders of a company. Executive committees and managing directors are only appointed if there is a board by its directors and require delegation of board powers.

SWEDEN

Limited Company (aktiebolag or AB) - A limited company (Aktiebolag or AB) is a separate and distinct legal entity. Managed by a board of directors, which is responsible for making major business decisions and overseeing general affairs of a company. Directors are elected by shareholders of an AB. The managing director (optional in private ABs and required in public ABs), who runs the day-to-day operations of an AB, is appointed by the board of directors. Other officers are appointed by the board of directors or by the managing director.

Trading Partnership (handelsbolag, HB) - Under the Partnership and Non-registered Partnership Act (Handelsbolagslagen), a trading partnership (Handelsbolag or HB) is constituted by an agreement between two or more individuals and/or legal entities to conduct business in an association. The most frequently cited advantage of the HB is its flexibility. Partners are free to organize their relations as they see fit without the restraints of a corporate form. Within the framework of an HB, complex structures can be set up to allow for many different characteristics and circumstances. The partners in an HB are personally liable for the partnership's agreements and debts.

Limited Partnership (kommanditbolag or KB) - A limited partnership (Kommanditbolag or KB) is a form of a trading partnership in which one or more partners have reserved the right not to be liable for the obligations of a KB in excess of the sum they have contributed or undertaken to contribute to a KB. Such a partner is referred to as a limited partner (Kommanditdelägare). Other partners in a KB are referred to as general partners (Komplementär). A KB must have two or more partners, at least one general partner, and one limited partner. The partnership's most frequently cited advantage is its flexibility. Partners are free to organize their relations as they see fit without the restraints of a corporate form. Within the framework of a partnership, complex structures can be set up to allow for many different characteristics and circumstances.

Branch office (filial, Branch) - A branch (Filial) is the branch office of a foreign company with a separate management in Sweden. A branch is not a separate legal entity. A foreign company may only have one branch in Sweden. A branch has no independent capital, and its assets and liabilities are a part of the total assets of the foreign company.

SWITZERLAND

Stock Corporation - This legal form is intended for large-sized companies with high capital requirements but is also popular among smaller companies. It is managed by a board of directors, which is elected by the general meeting of shareholders. The articles of incorporation may limit the transferability of a company's shares.

TAIWAN, CHINA

Company Limited by Shares - A company limited by shares must carry on a profit-seeking business and is a separate and distinct legal entity whereby its capital is divided into shares. A foreign investor must file a foreign investment application (FIA) with the Investment

Commission and, upon approval, incorporate an FIA company in Taiwan.

Closely-Held Company Limited by Shares - On June 15, 2015, a special section entitled "Closely-Held Company" (CHC) was added to Chapter 5 (Company Limited by Shares) as a result of the amendments to the Company Act.

Its purpose is to encourage the growth of startups and small and medium enterprises and to accommodate the unique needs of tech startups.

The amendments aim to create more autonomy for those small or medium companies and to increase the flexibility in CHC's share ownership arrangements and business operations.

Limited Company - A limited company is owned by members whose respective ownerships are stated in terms of the amount of the member's capital contributions. A foreign investor must file an FIA with the Investment Commission and, upon approval, incorporate a limited company in Taiwan. A limited company has fewer corporate formalities than a company limited by shares. For example, a limited company does not have shareholders' meetings.

Branch Office of a Foreign Company - A foreign company may register a branch office to carry out profit-seeking activities in Taiwan. A branch office is exempt from almost all of the corporate formality requirements of a company limited by shares.

THAILAND

Private Limited Company - Separate and distinct legal entity. It is managed by a board of directors, which is responsible for making major business decisions and overseeing the general affairs of a company. Directors are elected by the shareholders of a company.

Public Limited Company - Separate and distinct legal entity. It is managed by a board of directors, which is responsible for making major business decisions and overseeing the general affairs of a company. Directors are elected by the shareholders of a company. A public limited company can be newly incorporated or converted from, or amalgamated with, an existing private limited company. Usually, the purpose of using a public limited company is to obtain investment from the public at large, for example, by making a public offering of its shares.

Partnerships - There are three types of partnerships - Unregistered ordinary partnership (all partners are jointly and severally liable), Registered ordinary partnership (a partnership becomes a legal entity, separate and distinct from individual partners; all partners are jointly and severally liable for all obligations of a partnership), and Limited partnership (partnership becomes a legal entity, separate and distinct from individual partners). Limited partnerships are comprised of 2 types of partners - Partner(s) whose liability is limited to the amount of their capital contribution and Partners who are jointly and unlimitedly liable for all obligations of a partnership.

TURKEY

Joint-Stock Company (JSC) - A capital company with a legal personality. The general assembly of shareholders is the highest decision-making body in a JSC. The power to manage the business and affairs of a JSC is vested in its board members. Board members act as a corporate body and may have one or more members. Board members are not required to have a share in the company. Board members can transfer their duties and authority to one or more directors or a third party.

Limited Liability Company (LLC) - Capital Company with a legal personality. The general assembly of partners is the ultimate decision-making body in LLC. Management rights and duties of LLC are conferred to the managers. At least one partner must have management rights and representation power of an LLC as a manager. It is also possible to appoint third-party individuals who are not partners of the LLC as managers.

Other Business Forms Branch Offices (BO) - BOs may carry out the business their principal company is conducting and freely enjoy the right to pursue commercial activities. A foreign principal company remains liable for all debts of the BO. BOs have autonomous capital and accounting to carry out commercial transactions with third parties, although they are closely associated with the principal company in respect of internal management. This means that the rights, debts, profits, and losses of the BOs are assumed by the principal company. A BO can only engage in the activities of its principal company. Although there is no legal capital requirement for BOs, the principal company is required to maintain sufficient capital to run the BO in practice.

Liaison Offices (LO) - LO can only provide "representation" and "relationship management" with respect to the overseas principal company's Turkish customers and suppliers, but it cannot engage in any commercial or trading activity.

UKRAINE

The below summary provides an overview of 2 corporate structures that are commonly used in Ukraine. Other alternatives provided by law, such as private enterprise, additional liability company, general partnership, and limited partnership, may be used but are less common due to their legal uncertainty and additional liability for their participants.

It is also possible for a foreign company to establish a representative office, which, however, is not a separate company and the parent company remains liable for all obligations of such representative office.

Limited Liability Company (LLC)

1. Separate and distinct legal entity subject to certain exceptions; participants (shareholders) are not liable for debts and obligations of the company

2. Taxed on its earnings at a corporate level and participants taxed on any distributed dividends

3. Management and organization governed by charter (articles of association) and internal Director (board of directors) has overall management responsibility.

4. The LLC director is obliged to annually file information with the state registrar regarding LLC's ownership structure and ultimate beneficial owners and

5. Event-driven filings must be made from time to time, such as in the case of changes of director(s), ultimate beneficial owners or other corporate details; accuracy of information on the ultimate beneficial owners should be confirmed each time when the filing is made.

Joint-Stock Company (JSC)

1. Distinct legal entity separated from its shareholders. Subject to certain exceptions, shareholders are not liable for debts and obligations of the company

2. The law provides for 2 types of JSCs: public and private. The main differences between the two types of JSCs are:

   i. Shares of public JSCs are publicly traded on stock exchanges, while shares of private JSCs are placed among a limited number of persons

   ii. Shareholders of public JSCs do not have a pre-emptive right to purchase shares of a shareholder intending to alienate them to a third party. Charter of a private JSC can provide for such right

iii. When convening the general shareholders' meeting, in addition to notifications to shareholders, on own website and in the public database of the National Securities and Stock Market Commission (the Securities Commission), public JSCs shall also notify the stock exchange where its shares are traded

iv. Establishment of a supervisory board in public JSCs is mandatory

v. Members of the supervisory board of a public JSC are elected only through cumulative voting, and the minimum number of members is 5

vi. Mandatory establishment of an

a) Audit committee,

b) Remuneration committee and

c) Appointment committee in the supervisory board of a public JSC and

vii. When considering a prior approval for execution of a related party transaction, the supervisory board of a public JSC shall engage an independent auditor, and, if approved, publish the essential terms of such transaction.

3. JSC is a less common form than LLC as it has more regulated corporate procedures and less flexibility in adopting corporate decisions. In addition, the law provides for more strict and extensive reporting and notification procedures, including to the Securities Commission

4. Taxed on its earnings at a corporate level and shareholders taxed on any distributed dividends

5. Will be obliged to annually file information to the companies register regarding its ownership structure and ultimate beneficial owners as soon as secondary legislation is adopted

6. Must file annual report to the Securities Commission, which is publicly available.

7. Event-driven filings must be made from time to time, such as in the case changes of members of executive and supervisory bodies or other corporate details; during all such filings accuracy of information on the ultimate beneficial owners should be confirmed each time when the filing is made.

The regulation of JSC activities may be subject to change under the new law.

UNITED ARAB EMIRATES

The most commonly adopted legal structures in mainland UAE are limited liability companies (LLC) and branch offices (Branches). In addition, it is also possible to establish a representative office (also known as a liaison office), which is a legal structure identical to that of a Branch.

However, its activities are limited to serving as an administrative and marketing center for the parent company (Rep Office).

It is also possible to establish an entity in 1 of the free zones in the UAE. Entities registered in a free zone can be wholly foreign-owned, and no UAE participation is required. The free zone entity can take the form of a free zone limited liability company (FZ-LLC) or a free zone branch office (FZ-Branch).

LLC - Separate and distinct legal entity with limited liability. On November 23, 2020, the UAE government issued a new decree amending the Commercial Companies Law (New Law) to abolish the fundamental requirement of having 51 percent or UAE national ownership of an onshore company. Therefore, subject to the competent licensing authorities' specific requirements, LLCs may now be 100 percent owned by foreign shareholders.

A further notice- It is mooted that a further Strategic Impact Activities has been issued, which applies at a federal level to all Emirates (Cabinet Decision).

The Cabinet Resolution is expected during the 1st quarter. The strategic list broadly includes the following sectors:

i.   Security and defense activities and activities of a military nature
ii.   Banks, money-changing establishments, finance companies, and insurance activities
iii. Printing cash currency
iv.   Telecommunications
v.   Hajj and Umrah services
vi.   Holy Quran memorization centres
vii. Fishery-related services

Following the new Cabinet Resolution Decision, the competent licensing authorities in each Emirate have the discretion to establish the conditions for allowing increased foreign ownership in business activities not listed above as strategically restricted. The licensing authorities of each Emirate will, therefore, determine the permitted foreign ownership threshold of each business activity (not on the strategic list) and also set any other applicable requirements, such as minimum share capital or Emiratization thresholds.

Branch - A branch is not regarded as a separate entity but treated as an extension of its parent company. Currently, pursuant to the recent changes in the UAE law, a branch no longer requires a UAE national or a company wholly owned by UAE nationals to act as its national agent (colloquially known as a "sponsor" and is not to be confused with a commercial agent), subject to the implementation of the New Law which, amongst other things, has abolished this requirement.

The national agent provides licensing and other governmental services for the Branch for a fixed fee to be paid at the date of the licensee issuance but would not have any rights or entitlements to the Entity's business.

FZ-LLC - Separate and distinct legal entity with limited liability. There is no restriction on the nationality of shareholders. Activities restricted to the free zone in which the company is incorporated and those the company is licensed to carry out.

FZ-Branch: A branch is not regarded as a separate entity but treated as an extension of its parent company. There is no requirement to appoint a national agent as in the case of a Branch.

Dual License Branch: A Dual License Branch is a branch of an FZ-LLC established in mainland UAE. It is not treated as a separate entity but as an extension of its parent company. Establishing a dual licensee branch is possible in the case of FZ-LLCs registered only in certain free zones. It may operate from the same office as its parent company without the need for a separate registered address.

UNITED KINGDOM

Private limited company - Separate and distinct legal entity. Managed by directors who are responsible for making major decisions and overseeing the general affairs of the company. Subject to the articles of the company, the shareholders and the board of directors generally have the power to appoint and remove directors.

Public Limited Company - A further alternative is a public limited company, which is a company limited by shares or guarantees. This form of entity could be useful in some instances (as, unlike a private limited company, it enables capital to be raised from the public), but as it is a less commonly used type of company, it is not covered in this guide.

Limited Liability Partnership - Distinct legal entity separate from its members. Subject to certain exceptions (such as fraud), members are not liable for debts and obligations of the company. It provides flexibility in management and organization. A confidential LLP agreement governs management and organization. Designated members are responsible for specific statutory requirements (such as signing annual accounts). An LLP must have two designated members carrying on a lawful business with a view of profit.

Registered UK Establishment - A registered UK establishment is a UK registration of an overseas company. It has no separate legal personality from the overseas company. The overseas company continues to be managed by the directors and shareholders of the overseas company.

VIETNAM

Vietnamese corporate laws introduce five entity types: a joint stock company (JSC), a limited liability company with two or more members (LLC2), a limited liability company with one member (LLC1), a partnership, and a private enterprise. The LLC1 is the most popular and widely used type by foreign investors when they intend to set up and wholly own and control a legal entity in Vietnam. Partnerships and private enterprises are more suitable for local and small investors. In addition, the form of partnership may only be designed and appropriate for a limited number of specific professional businesses, such as legal or auditing businesses. Therefore, we will only cover the first three entity types: JSC, LLC2, and LLC1.

Joint Stock Company (JSC)

• At least, 3 shareholders and no restriction to the maximum number.

• Generally, no personal financial liability of shareholders as it is limited to their capital contribution in a JSC.

• Earnings of a company are subject to corporate income tax and shareholders (only individuals) are taxed on any distributed dividends.

• Typical corporate documents generally include an Enterprise Registration Certificate (ERC), the charter (which is usually called the articles of incorporation in certain jurisdictions), organizational resolutions of the general shareholders meeting (GSM) and the board of management (BOM), shareholders' registration book and share certificates.

• The GSM makes decisions on the most important affairs of the JSC. The BOM has overall responsibility to implement the GSM's decisions and makes decisions on certain, less important affairs of the JSC. The general director (or CEO) has day-to-day management responsibilities.

• Shareholders typically purchase shares in the JSC, either ordinary shares or preference shares.

• Individual shareholders are required to file tax returns (personal income tax) with local tax authorities upon receiving dividends (where they would like to declare tax by themselves). With respect to corporate shareholders, the distributed dividends would be included in their tax finalization returns (corporate income tax) at the end of the relevant fiscal year.

Limited Liability Company with 2 Or More Members (LLC2)

• Must have at least 2 members and no more than 50; can be both individuals and legal entities

- Generally, no personal financial liability of members as it is limited to their capital contributions in an LLC2.

- Earnings of a company are subject to corporate income tax and members (only individuals) are taxed on any distributed profits.

- Typical corporate documents generally include:

- Enterprise Registration Certificate (ERC)

- Charter (which is usually called articles of incorporation in certain jurisdictions)

- Organizational resolutions of the Members' Council (MC)

- Members registration books and

- Capital contribution certificates

- The MC makes decisions on the most important affairs of the LLC2 and has overall management responsibility. General Director (or CEO) has day-to-day management responsibilities.

- Members contribute capital to the charter capital of LLC2 or purchase paid capital contributions from former members.

- Individual members are required to file tax returns (personal income tax) with local tax authorities upon receiving profits (where they would like to declare tax by themselves). With respect to corporate members, the distributed profits would be included in their tax finalization returns (corporate income tax) at the end of the relevant fiscal year.

Limited Liability Company with 1 Member (LLC1)

- Only 1 member is required, either an individual or a legal entity.

- Generally, no personal financial liability of a member as it is limited to its capital contribution in an LLC1.

- Company's earnings are subject to corporate income tax, but the sole member (either a corporate or an individual) is not taxed on any distributed profits.

- Typical corporate documents generally include:
  o Enterprise Registration Certificate (ERC)

- o Charter (usually called the articles of incorporation in certain jurisdictions) and
- o Decisions of the sole member, which may be made directly by a member or indirectly through either the member's council or the company president.

• Either the member's council or the company president has overall management responsibility. The General Director (or CEO) has day-to-day management responsibility.

• Member contributes capital to the charter capital of the LLC1 or purchase paid capital contribution from the former member.

• Where the company owner is a legal entity, its distributed profits would be included in its tax finalization return (corporate income tax) at the end of the relevant fiscal year.

Partnership

• At least 2 unlimited liability partners (only individuals) and no restriction to the maximum number; no restriction to the minimum and maximum number of limited liability partners.

• Generally, no personal financial liability of limited liability partners as it is limited in their capital contributions in the partnership. However, unlimited liability partners are liable for the obligations of the partnership to the extent of all of their assets.

• Earnings of a partnership are subject to corporate income tax and partners (only individuals) are taxed on any distributed profits.

• Typical corporate documents generally include Enterprise Registration Certificate (ERC), charter (which is usually called articles of incorporation in certain jurisdictions), decisions of the Partners' Council and capital contribution certificates.

• Partners' Council has overall management responsibilities; unlimited liability partners have day-to-day management responsibilities.

- Partners contribute capital to the charter capital of a Partnership. The limited liability partners can purchase paid capital contribution in the Partnership from former limited liability partners.

- Individual partners are required to file tax returns (personal income tax) with local tax authorities upon receiving profits (where they would like to submit a self-declaration of their tax). With respect to corporate limited liability partners, the distributed profits would be included in their tax finalization returns (corporate income tax) at the end of the relevant fiscal year.

Private enterprise

- Only a sole individual owner
- The owner has personal liability for all activities of the private enterprise to the extent of all of their assets.
- Earnings of an enterprise are subject to corporate income tax, but the sole individual owner is not taxed on any distributed profits
- Typical corporate documents generally include an Enterprise Registration Certificate (ERC) and internal rules issued by the owner.
- Owner has overall and day-to-day management responsibilities.
- Owner registers the investment capital of a private enterprise.

Authorized signatories/Board resolution

While doing business with large organizations, it is recommended to understand the hierarchy of the organization and to understand whom to reach out to in case of any emergencies or for any specific intervention. It would also be essential to obtain documents like Board resolutions or Power of attorney, etc, authorizing particular individuals who may be authorized to conduct business on behalf of the organization.

Other aspects (such as insolvency)

As the business environment is getting complex, there is another aspect that would need to be understood before getting into the contract and also during the execution of the project. This is to check if an organization is undergoing some financial stress, which has led to it being managed by a government authority or has been declared bankrupt.

Details of bankruptcy proceedings would usually be available on www.ibbi.in (for companies in India). Considering that construction contracts extend over longer periods of time, it is recommended to keep checking the status of the organizations that we do business with.

From the above discussions, it can be seen that apart from understanding the terms and conditions of the contract agreement, it is recommended to understand your Client, Contractor, or vendor with whom you wish to do business. Depending on the country, there are certain advantages and challenges. You are encouraged to review the details of your existing business relationships and evaluate the advantages and risks associated with each.

Call to Action:

The above list and details are only indicative. You are requested to consult the Finance and Legal professionals in your organization, geography, and in your respective industries to have a better understanding of the advantage and risks associated with the types of legal entities within your domain of works

CONCLUSION

In the business world, an important factor is the element of trust which leads to ease and comfort of doing business between the transacting individuals or organizations eventually leading to long term healthy business relationships. In order to ensure such long-term healthy business relationships, it becomes important to ensure that every business transaction is completed in a manner so as to ensure that there are no disputes (or the same is minimized). The success of every business depends on all elements of the transaction which are generally recorded through a contract agreement. It is hence necessary to understand all aspects of any transaction and capture the elements accurately within the contract agreement. Through this book, I have attempted to inform the readers of the various aspects of entering into a contract using the example of a construction contract. The elements forming part of a construction contract can be extended and /or modified to suit the requirements of any other transaction for any other industry. The important aspect is to have a good understanding of all aspects which will help all stakeholders to understand and negotiate the same with the business associates.

Further in order for young entrepreneurs and students to get a good understanding of the contracts, I have attempted to create an awareness of the standard forms of contract available for various aspects of construction contracts. These standard forms are published by various reputed international consulting organizations, various public sector organizations of various countries and by large multinational corporations as well. If you are new to any field, it is best to get started using existing standards which are available for use and later the same can be improvised to suit the specific requirements. The readers are encouraged to explore the standard forms of contracts available in their respective industries and geographies.

Lastly an attempt has been made to create an awareness about the various types of legal entities in India and few other countries and its repercussions while choosing your customer or service provider.

References

1. https://thorntonandlowe.com/
2. www.ijesi.org/papers/Vol(5)3/E0503029036.pdf
3. https://www.civillead.com/what-is-boq/)
4. (https://manufacturers.thenbs.com/resources/knowledge/15-reasons-why-specifications-are-still-important)
5. https://ppra.forumotion.com/t242-importances-of-specification
6. https://www.pinsentmasons.com/out-law/guides/programmes-of-works-and-construction-contracts
7. https://www.projectmanager.com/blog/project-management/planning-techniques-for-projects
8. https://www.designingbuildings.co.uk/wiki/Programme_for_building_design_and_construction
9. https://www.designingbuildings.co.uk/wiki/Expression_of_interest_for_construction_contracts
10. https://www.artscapediy.org/guide/what-is-a-request-for-expressions-of-interest/
11. https://www.opcw.org/sites/default/files/documents/2020/02/General%20Instructions%20for%20Bidders.pdf
12. https://harperjames.co.uk/article/boilerplate-clauses-in-commercial-contracts/
13. https://tremblylaw.com/8-common-boilerplate-clauses-and-why-they-matter/
14. https://blog.ipleaders.in/overlook-boilerplate-clauses/
15. https://www.mondaq.com/india/corporate-and-company-law/225570/status-check--boilerplate-clauses
16. https://www.upcounsel.com/boilerplate-clauses-in-commercial-contracts
17. https://blog.ipleaders.in/overlook-boilerplate-clauses/
18. https://hallellis.co.uk/boilerplate-clauses-law/

19. https://www.lawteacher.net/free-law-essays/contract-law/standard-forms-of-construction-contracts-contract-law-essay.php
20. https://www.mondaq.com/india/corporatecommercial-law/272948/law-related-to-standard-form-of-contracts
21. https://sociallawstoday.com/standard-form-of-contract-all-about-it/
22. https://lawexplores.com/fidic/
23. https://www.dlapiperrealworld.com/law/index.html?t=co nstruction&s=forms-of-contract-procurement-methods
24. https://aaqs.org/local-agreements/
25. http://corbett.co.uk
26. www.mca.gov.in
27. https://nnroad.com/blog/types-of-business-entities-in-india/
28. https://www.dlapiperintelligence.com/goingglobal/corpor ate/index.html?t=01-form-of-entity
29. www.fidic.org
30. www.neccontract.com
31. www.iccwbo.org
32. www.jctltd.co.uk

ABOUT THE AUTHOR

As a construction management professional, Manish Mohandas has extensive experience in various functions related to construction such as construction management, commercial management, and procurement.

He has worked on projects including plotted developments, affordable housing, villas, and high-rise buildings in Abu Dhabi, Dubai, Mumbai, Bangalore, Chennai, Maldives, and Colombo.

His career spans roles at companies like VMS Consultants, Mumbai India, Hindustan Construction Company (HCC India), ETA ASCON (UAE), ALDAR Laing O'Rourke (UAE), Rustomjee Group in Mumbai, Tata Housing (Mumbai, Bangalore, Colombo, and Maldives), and recently with Karle Group in Bangalore.

Apart from core responsibilities, Manish has led and worked on contracts utilizing FIDIC 1999 (Red Book), NEC contracts, ICTAD forms of contract in Sri Lanka, and various bespoke contracts.

He has also been associated with the Project Management Institute, USA (PMI) since August 2019, thoroughly enjoying interactions with his fellow professionals.

www.ingramcontent.com/pod-product-compliance
Lightning Source LLC
Chambersburg PA
CBHW032039080426
42733CB00006B/133